OUTSOURCING
MAINTENANCE

SCALING BETWEEN
TOP LINE & BOTTOM LINE

I0480117

Ajay Srivastava

INDIA · SINGAPORE · MALAYSIA

Notion Press

No.8, 3rd Cross Street
CIT Colony, Mylapore
Chennai, Tamil Nadu – 600004

First Published by Notion Press 2020
Copyright © Ajay Srivastava 2020
All Rights Reserved.

ISBN 978-1-64951-602-2

Dedication

I dedicate this book, OUTSOURCING MAINTENANCE – Scaling between the top line and bottom line, to the millions of you in industries on customer side as Maintenance team at floor, OHS, Contract cell, SCM, HR etc. from different industries and a whole lot of service provider including Facility Management, Asset Management, and Plant maintenance. Etc.

At the time when all of us are worse affected by the current pandemic crisis and feeling somewhat helpless and uncertain about the coming times. I want you to know that these are, despite what they may seem, the best time to add on the business view of maintenance services across the horizon to give clarity on contract management in a dizzy atmosphere all around.

I am sure this book, like others, will give you a clear picture of the entire outsourcing business as a whole. I have made a conscious effort to limit the word as the entire book can be written on each topic. The objective of this book is to provide you with the insight on the ever-changing situation in addition to assigned direct responsibility. Once you understand the truth of the complete business model having bird's eye view, you will be able to maneuver your career successfully within the industry and beyond.

Contents

Preface

This book grows on you. I know because it grew on me. In my career journey through different industries interacting with different people throughout the entire hierarchy vertical and horizontal, obviously each coming from a different school of thought. In my active career span of more than two decade, I find myself always on the opposite side of the flow i.e. being with the customer at the time when OEM were more resourceful & running the show with monopolistic business model and by when I changed the side, the situation was altogether reversed. It was somewhat like AC motor by the time direction of current change in the rotor; it is moved to the opposite pole keeping motor rotating.

I witnessed a time when, many of the Hardcore engineering company searching grounds in landscaping & other low skill jobs making the outsourcing business not only cost effective but also customer centric. As by then customer started thinking of limiting no. of contractors, with all contracts managed under a single umbrella contract. Initially the maintenance contract of specialized plants were usually executed by the OEM's and process specialist, whereas facility management, and other soft services were executed separately by local contractors in isolation. However, with time, the boundaries dissolved and each becomes a synonym of each other.

With the advancement of time and technology upgrade, the major shift, which we all come across, is the technical skills and subject expertise, which shifted from big industries/OEM to Individual SME's and system houses causing a complete transformation in the way the service business was executed. It has been good for the growth of economy & society as whole and these new emerging entrepreneurs and business houses were now vendors for the company/OEMs from where they originated.

In the Industries, I realize all new entrants with adequate subject knowledge and filled with aspiration & energy to grow remain focus on their area of control and job responsibilities. This approach sometimes deviates from organization goal which is about sustaining business and that inspired me to put forward this book. This book is a small step towards summarising different aspects of outsourcing maintenance as guide for new entrants in industry and reference book for veteran to review the subject as a whole to ensure,nothing is missed out.

The information expressed herein is known to most of the industrial professional and vividly available in public domain has been summarized, with blend of day-to-day experience covering all perspective of contract management as relevant to plant maintenance. You may find few points like vendor selection, Risks etc. repetitively as I have taken up the subject from three perspective i.e. Customer, Service provider & Contract between them. In addition to this, there are multiple industries with different culture & priorities. The values figures and graphs used are not actual or up to the scale, but only indicative for better understanding.

In the current fast-moving time, I strongly believe that everyone and anyone in any profession to keep the update of a holistic business situation, with all its components, and changing national and international environment. The COVID 19 crisis is a recent example of the same, as is expected to bring many visible and invisible changes between pre and post-crisis times.

I'm often asked," Well, if you could distill advice to a single sentence, what would it be?" I'd say," It is all about making end customer successful and delighted," and that is all what you get with these pages. Enjoy them.

– **Ajay Srivastava**

Chapter 1

Maintenance Outsourcing – An Introduction

"Still, history is the long process of outsourcing human ability in order to leverage more of it."

– Richard Powers

Introduction

Outsourcing is not a new term and continues to co-exist since the evolution of mankind, although forms keep on changing with changing civilization and its needs. Way back in ancient time hunting was the only mean for survival. Later with development in agriculture and adoption of farming by some tribes, give rise to conflict. This might have finally given way to the first agreement of those times. The people adopting agriculture shared the yield with hunting tribes, which in turn agreed to give protection to farmers and crops from wild animals.

Taking another example from our ancestors where they use to live in the joint family working on agriculture farms. Males in family use to work in farms and females use to take care of house chores with responsibility among them specifically delegated among women in the house, somewhat similar to industries. With the change in time joint family splitting into nuclear families with similar arrangement males responsible for earning and women of the house taking care of children and other house chores.

With improving lifestyle causing an increase in expenses with widespread education, both the family member took up for earning and day to day activities like cleaning, dishwashing, etc. outsourced to domestic help. It was never a matter of quality of the job, but the objective remains to take over high-value jobs by the lady at home and home maids despite their limited education could aid in improved financial stature of their family.

We come across wide range of examples in our everyday life i.e. from general skills Personal grooming at Saloon, car cleaning, cobbler, and electrician to specialized service such as Car repair, Job consultancy, and finance advisor to Health consultant. If we look into the activities like Car driver, car cleaning and car repair are associated with same equipment but service requirement, Work scope, KPI and pricing model are different.

Even in current time of COVID-19 crisis and country wide lock down people took over many general activity as person grooming, car cleaning etc. but how many of us had really tried our hands on car repair or self medication. I do not think there will be many, as in such case, risk involved is high.

Industrial Context

Industrial context also remains similar i.e. initially automobile companies like ford were owning entire set up from mines to the final car but later car manufacturers come up with vendors supplying different components. This practice is evident even today but further extended to the outsourcing of the entire manufacturing process. Here outsourcing not only increased efficiency but also the flexibility by large as ford initially could supply a single model with no color choice.

The growth in outsourcing in recent years is partly the result of a general shift in business philosophy. Before the mid-1980s, many organizations sought to acquire other organizations and diversify their business interests to reduce risk. As more organizations discovered that there were limited advantages to running a large group of unrelated businesses, many began to divest subsidiaries and refocus their efforts on one or a few closely related areas of business. Organizations began to identify or develop core competencies, a unique combination of experience and expertise that would provide a source of competitive advantage in a given industry. All aspects of the organization's operations were aligned around the core competence, and any activities or functions that were not considered necessary to preserve it were then outsourced.

Classification of core and non – core activities continued to be a never-ending debate based on industrial culture or personal preferences. Successful outsourcing requires a strong understanding of the organization's capabilities and future direction. Decisions regarding outsourcing significant functions are among the most strategic that can be made by an organization; because they address the basic organizational choice of the functions for which internal expertise is developed and nurtured and those for which such expertise is purchased. These are basic decisions regarding organizational design. Outsourcing based only upon a comparison of costs can lead organizations to miss opportunities to gain innovative solutions that might lead to the development of new products or technologies. Organizations that outsource too many of their core functions are often referred to as "hollow organizations" and may relinquish their reason for existence.

Outsourcing can be undertaken in varying degrees, ranging from total outsourcing to selective outsourcing. Total outsourcing may involve dismantling entire departments or divisions and transferring the employees, facilities, equipment, and complete responsibility for a product or function to an outside vendor. In contrast, selective outsourcing may target a single, time-consuming task within a department, such as preparing the payroll or manufacturing a minor component, which can be handled more efficiently by an outside specialist. The opposite of outsourcing is in sourcing when a staff function within an organization markets its product or service to external as well as internal customers.

The outsourcing of complete manufacturing is brought into practice even today in various industries like pharmacy, API, textiles, etc. Organizations that decide to outsource do so for several reasons. The primary reason is to achieve cost savings or to better cost control over the outsourced function. Organizations usually outsource to a vendor that specializes in a given function and performs that function more efficiently.

Anticipated cost savings sometimes fail to materialize, however, because the vendor must make a profit and because the organization incurs additional transaction costs when interacting with a vendor. Another common reason for outsourcing is to achieve headcount reductions or minimize the fluctuations in staffing that may occur due to changes in demand for a product or service. Organizations also Outsource to reduce the workload on their employees or to provide more development opportunities for their employees by freeing them from tedious tasks.

Some organizations outsource to eliminate distractions and force themselves to concentrate on their core competencies. Still, others outsource to achieve greater financial flexibility, since the sale of assets that formerly supported an outsourced function can improve cash flow. A possible pitfall in this reasoning is that many vendors demand long-term contracts, which may reduce flexibility. A common reason for outsourcing computer programming and other information technology functions is to gain access to new technology and outside expertise. Some experts claim, however, that organizations are exposed to new technology by vendors anyway, and that they could simply hire people with the expertise they seek. Organizational politics is another common reason for outsourcing. For example, some organizations might begin outsourcing initiatives after observing the successful efforts of a competitor. Others might be pushed toward outsourcing by managers seeking personal gain or by a desire to eliminate troublesome departments. Finally, outsourcing provides an attractive option for manufacturing firms as they grow.

Some of the major potential disadvantages to outsourcing include poor quality control, decreased organization loyalty, a lengthy bid process, and a loss of strategic alignment. There may also be inherent advantages of maintaining certain functions internally. For example, employees may have a better understanding of the industry, and their vested interests may mean they are more likely to make decisions following the organization's goals. A general rule is that an organization should never outsource any function that directly affects the quality of service.

Once an organization has decided to outsource, there are still several factors it must consider in making a successful transition and forming a partner relationship with the vendor. First, the organization needs to obtain the support of key personnel for the decision to outsource. Many organizations encounter resistance from employees who feel that their jobs are threatened by outsourcing. However thoroughly professional team comprising of an outsourcing expert, representatives from senior management and human resources, and the managers of all affected areas of the organization to help address employee concerns about the decision. Then the organization can begin contacting potential vendors, either formally or informally, and asking specific questions about the services provided and the terms of the contract. It is also important for the organization to develop tangible measures of job performance before entering into an agreement. Finally, the organization should select a vendor it trusts in order to develop a mutually beneficial partner relationship. Some of the possible advantages can be expected of outsourcing are as:

- cost reduction, through economies of scale,
- cash influx through liquidation of assets and decrease in depreciation expense,
- Access to technology without capital investment, and
- Elimination of a large cost center within the organization and transfer to profit center within vendors Operation.

Possible drawbacks to outsourcing are:

- Loss of control,
- High exit barriers,
- Conversion costs,
- increased executive management involvement,
- Dependence on vendor reliability,
- Concerns with long-term flexibility,

- Ability to meet changing needs, and
- service-level contract agreements with outsource service provider.

Outsourcing is a very common practice today. Both small and large organizations are adopting these practices by evaluating Benefits and drawbacks in their context.

Types of Outsourcing

As per the specific individual & industrial requirement different service outsourcing models are as –

1. Manufacturing Outsourcing
2. Visit based Service Outsourcing
3. Consulting & Engineering services
4. Maintenance services
5. At individual level jobsites, Marriage sites, Stock consultancy etc.

Sway Between Top Line and Bottom Line

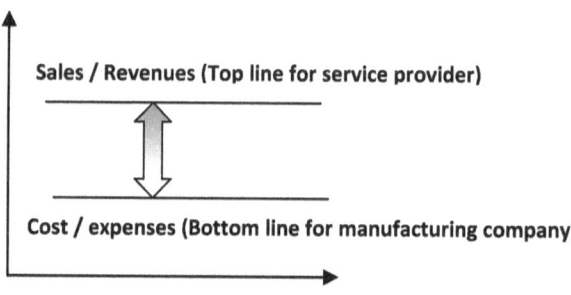

Fig – I

The dissent between Client and Service provider lies with their difference in business objective as client is working out possibility for improving bottom line with reducing cost of ownership, improving margins and beating competition. Here bottom line comprise of "3 P" as People, Plant Equipment and Profits.

On other hand service provider focus on improvement in top line by increasing sales by pumping more and more resources and services into the contract. For OEM's these contracts can be an opportunity to boost the product sales.

As depicted from the figure-I best point for operation, establish at the point striking chord between client and service provider. Although Customer requirement are independent but needs to be realistic. Service provider is dependent on customer with priorities aligned towards business enhancement.

Mismatching Visions (Service Providers vs. Customers)

When the provider is a pioneer in providing services by Performance contracts, some of its customers may be reluctant to make the shift, saying that "we've always done our maintenance, we are in control, we don't want to give you control, we feel we are losing something", so the negotiation becomes very difficult. Lack of alignment in visions also means that the service provider and the customer have different visions regarding the nature of Performance contracts and nature of the relationships. From some providers' perspective, the importance of Performance contracts is to set practical ground rules for implementations and to build a collaborative relationship. While some customers still think in a traditional way, considering the contracts as rigid agreements without flexibility. In that sense, every time when a problem rises, the Service provider thinks to work together with the customer to solve the problem, while the customer thinks to go back to the contract and ends up in a contract review. When customers are not fully into the concept of Performance contracts, they don't consider the Service provider as a partner and don't work together with the Service provider with openness and in the spirit of partnership. So gaps in visions on servitization, on the nature of Performance contracts and on the nature of the relationships lead to both commercial risk at the contracting stage and operational risk at the implementation stage.

This can be very well understood by an example as:

Customer usually in RFQ illustrates the nos. of people required, with competency level. The criterion here for competency is Qualification and years of experience. In case of some special skills say machine turner the customer looking to his job requirement asks for ITI with 10 yrs. Experience. Let us assume that minimum salary (as per local job market) meeting this criterion comes to around Rs. 60,000/ – Per month. Service provider in an attempt to get this order search out for the person meeting the criteria way below the normal market price bracket, which may later turn into disaster.

This can be case for any role, but turns to be critical when position requires direct machine exposure, which may lead to Equipment damage, system failure or even fatality.

Please be aware the above example should not be misunderstood, concluding "outsourcing model with cost plus margin "as a better model. Cost plus basis model is always advantage to service provider, as it frees him from any cost control effort keeping his margin intact.

Maintenance Outsourcing is now a day widely practiced in India, However different approaches can be broadly categorized as:

1. Asset Management – Equipment Focused approach

2. Exploiting to maximum approach – Production/yield centered approach

3. Keep running approach – Management strategic decision

Asset Management – The basic objective here is to maintain equipment well as per OEM recommendation. Customer in this approach looks for expert services preferably OEM'S to cater their facility to retain system availability at maximum assuring best possible productivity. The customer criterion for this type of maintenance is-

*   Capital investment in term of Cost of Plant/Equipment is extremely huge.

*   Periodic process.

*   Every equipment is considered as an asset.

*   Equipment maintained in line with OEM recommendation.

*   Enhanced Equipment life with minimal erosion to equipment condition.

- Medical equipment in hospitals, Government public sector, Power plants or process equipment with complex technologies are into these categories.

Exploiting to Maximum approach – This is basically Yield/Production centered approach with objective being drawing highest productivity. Either plants are very old or being into seasonal business customer may intend to run plant at overrated capacity with some equipment overloaded. The customer criterion for this type of maintenance is-

- Customer production here is into highly profitable business and any outage may lead to major loss.

- Customer process is complicated with large time/cost or both is involved to restart the system after once gone into shutdown.

- Looking into criticality customer will not mind to pay extra buck as premium to ensure trouble free continuous system operation.

- Customer ready to spend to maintain redundancy for equipment and bit liberal in maintaining spare inventory.

- Customer would here insist to continuously run the plant rather than any process focused approach.

- CD & software component manufacturing, Cement & Glass plants belong to the category

Keep Running Approach – Outsourcing for convenience, Customer simply is not interested in doing non-core activities (non-productive job) and wishes to offload the same to anyone to keep the system running and focus himself to administration/production keeping cost in control. Most of the existing maintenance contract now a day falls in these categories. This is moreover a strategic approach. The customer criterion for this type of maintenance is-

- Applicable to batch process plants.

- Maintenance outsourcing here is a strategy.

- Management philosophy to employ minimum manpower and attaining hassle free operation.

- Minimum staff strength on company's role that too moreover for commercial or administrative function.

- Customer here sometime insists for OEM services to get hassle free approval from financial institute or insurance claim in case of miss happening.

- To minimize the complication of multipoint communication with contractor customer here insist to have umbrella contract to have single window communication for all the problems.

- FMCG & Automobile industry falls into the category.

Although above-mentioned are broadly classified categories and different contracts are fixed along with customer priority including mix criteria falling under different categories.

Functional Difference

Features	Asset Management	Exploiting to maximum	Keep running approach
Approach	System oriented	Organization/team oriented.	System oriented.
Technical competency requirement	Moderate, but strong back office support is available.	High technical competency, excellent process knowledge & good back up association with OEM at different levels.	No specialization is required, Suitable for day-to-day operation.
Commitment level	Limited to OEM recommendations.	Very high level of commitment	Minimal/No commitment.
Influence in customer decision	Govern customer decision on their product.	Having influence in customer decision, Command partnership position.	Minimal to low influence on customer decision.

Features	Asset Management	Exploiting to maximum	Keep running approach
Repeat order	Order repetition & extension is outcome of product monopoly of already installed equipment.	Order repetition & extension is outcome of merits and created history.	Order repetition & extension out of negotiation skills &relationship.
Work scope	Well defined	Sketchy demarcation of work scope. All complex engineering and process are assumed to be in scope.	Foggy demarcation of work scope. General defined scope with all activities and area in scope.
Price	Costly	Very expensive	Reasonably priced.

Role of Service provider:

Service provider may also deploy outsourcing under different models.

- Outsourcing to extend arm to tap more business spread in the market and enhance market share. Outsourcing agencies are moreover competent partner.

- Outsourcing to focus on core activity and rather shifting low value labor-intensive job to third party. Job here is executed under continuous & close supervision.

- Supplier does not have any resources, supplier act as integrator of different services of different vendors and service provider.

Risks and Un-certainties:

This is one more subject, which leads to never-ending discussion. Customer always insist to pass on the risk of asset to service provider , whereas service provider also tries to manage the uncertainties with appropriate risk mitigation plan and provision for exit through different disclaimers, exclusion clause, and finally limiting the liability to utmost the value of entire contract. In fact, it should be clear in mind "FINAL RESPONSIBILITY LIES WITH OWNER "and he should act accordingly.

It's like hiring a driver for your limousine, and in case of any accident/incident maximum accountability with driver shall be limited to one month salary or at the most you may discharge him from his services, but you cannot expect to recover the damages or repair cost from him.

In industrial context, also we come across similar situations. Say for example, responsibility of periodic draining water from fuel is within scope of some outsourced service provider. The helper assigned the job missed to close the drain water valve properly, causing it leakage and spillage to plant drain connecting to the common drain and polluting pond nearby causing environmental issues with lot of clamours from local public and Municipal authorities with FIR at local police station. Local villagers doing protest to close down of industry, claiming spilled chemical/fuel caused death of their cattle. Service provider in such case may suspend the employee or operation as whole. However, consequential effects are to be borne by end customer at location.

Who can forget the Bhopal gas tragedy with a Gas (MIC) leak incident on Night of 2–3rd December of 1984 at the union carbide pesticide plant (UCIL).

However, risk in term of cost can be shared with service partner in issues like inventory management etc. or in case of comprehensive contracts with spares supply in service provider scope.

Risk and uncertainty are different terms, but people tend to confuse them. Managing risks is easier because you can identify them and develop a response plan based on your experience. However, managing uncertainty is very difficult, as previous information is not available, too many parameters are involved, and you cannot predict the outcome. Examples of risks are already stated earlier, the recent crisis of COVID 19 pandemic is perfect example of uncertainty.

Differences Between Risk and Uncertainty

The following are a few differences between risk and uncertainty:

- In risk you can predict the possibility of a future outcome, while in uncertainty you cannot.

- Risks can be managed while uncertainty is uncontrollable.

- Risks can be measured and quantified while uncertainty cannot.

- You can assign a probability to risks events, while with uncertainty, you can't.

However, to complete your project successfully, you must be very cautious, proactive, and open-minded to manage risks and uncertainty.

Maintenance Process: Various Standards as applicable and associated with maintenance are as follows as to be adopted by service provider at site as per customer practice in line with Industry guidelines –

Maintenance standards incorporate proven methods to best perform tasks such as cleaning, lubrication, repairs, components' replacement, data collection and more. They can also instruct professionals on how to create comprehensive checklists of maintenance tasks, as well as on how to structure them into integrated maintenance programs.

Standards are useful when applied to technological systems. For example, they can be used to develop interoperable systems that can exchange data and services to boost the replication of maintenance solutions. Such data exchange and sharing is key to sharing visualizations across stakeholders and supporting new cost-effective ideas for remote maintenance. Standard based systems and processes provide a good industrial maintenance practices in a highly diverse landscape of different plants, equipment and processes.

These standards include both maintenance procedures and systems, including emerging network systems that are part of industry digitization. The latter systems have recently expanded the number and scope of maintenance related standards, since they have given rise to processes for collecting, processing and analyzing data. Service provider can use this strong database to explore different possibilities.

I. ISO 9001 Quality Management

1. **Resources**

   The Management Team considers the capabilities, constraints on internal resources when determining the, competency, and training requirements necessary for effective management, Service requirement, verification activities, including internal audits.

In addition, what resources need to be obtained from external providers will be taken into consideration. The Management Team will allocate adequate resources to achieve agreed KPI'S objectives and conformity service requirements. The methods used to identify and provide necessary resources include strategic planning, annual budget planning, weekly staff and production meetings. Management will communicate to all employees the relevance and importance of their work in contributing to the achievement of quality objectives and conformity to service requirements.

2. **People**

The Management Team will determine and provide personnel necessary for the effective implementation and operation of the Quality Management System processes

Determine competency requirements by role;

- Document competency requirements in the job description;

- Ensure personnel performing specific roles are qualified on the basis of appropriate education, training and/or experience;

- Evaluate an employee's competency through an annual management assessment and performance evaluation process;

- Take actions to acquire the necessary competence when gaps or needs are identified;

- Evaluate the effectiveness of action taken; and

- Retain records to provide evidence of competence.

All employees to be made aware of The Quality Policy as follows:

- Quality objectives and results;

- Their contribution to the effectiveness of the Quality Management System;

- The benefits of improved Quality System Management Performance;
- The significance of non-conformance with the Quality Management System requirement; and
- Safety procedures, goals and results.

3. **Infrastructure**

The Management Team identifies the infrastructure necessary to meet the needs of the business. Resources and personnel will be provided to develop and maintain the infrastructure to assure that customer's quality objectives and service requirements are achieved. The Infrastructure includes:

- Office area, workshop, Storage and associated utilities;
- Process equipment, including both hardware and software;
- Supporting services like transportation vehicle, Guest house facility; and
- Communications and information technology. Consideration will be made for environmental issues associated with the infrastructure such as conservation, waste, and pollution and recycling as required.

4. **Environment for the Maintenance Processes**

Management Team shall determine, provide and manage the environment that is suitable for the operation to achieve, quality objectives and conformity to product requirements. Factors considered determining the type of environment required is based on the:

- Industry type, social and psychological needs;
  - Documentation & Records of SOP, SMP, Maintenance schedules
  - Equipment test process & Reports. Alarming parameters identified with necessary action plan.
  - Periodic reports i.e. Daily Monthly and annual report.

- Processing performed in the location i.e. devising and review equipment checklists.

- Tools, Tackles, PPE, Consumable etc. requirements;

- Level of skill, number of employee working in the area;

- Type of environmental conditions, e.g. lighting, heat, humidity, sound levels, and air quality;

- Risk associated with processing or equipment operation (Safety); and

- Ergonomics.

5. **Safety procedure**

The Management Team identifies and establishes safety initiatives. Site In charge coordinates safety initiatives under guidelines laid by HO. Safety inspections are conducted to identify unsafe work conditions. The Emergency Response Team performs safety inspections, findings are recorded on form Customer Safety and Housekeeping Worksheet.

Issues identified during safety inspection are recorded and findings and action are reported to Management. All personnel are expected to report work environment changes to Management that could result in unsafe conditions that may inhibit the ability to achieve objectives or conformity to product requirements. Corrective action shall be taken to restore the work environment back to its intended function. The following Operating Procedures define the requirements to assure that infrastructure and environment will allow site team to achieve organization objectives broadly on following lines-

- Lockout/Tag-out Procedure

- General Machine Guarding Requirements for all Machines

- Safety Policy and Procedures for complete Plant

- Human Resources (Competence, training and awareness)

- Preservation of Equipment including Monsoon protection (Handling – Storage &Packaging)

6. **Measurement Traceability**

All equipment used for inspection, measuring and testing of products is identified and calibrated under suitable environmental conditions, at prescribed intervals with traceability to measurement standard provided by the National Institute of Standards and Technology. When standards do not exist, record for the basis used for calibration will be retained.

The process employed for calibration is defined by Work Instructions and the Equipment Control Database. These include the equipment:

- Type,
- Identification,
- Location,
- Frequency of checks,
- Check method, and
- Acceptance criteria.

Calibration stickers are stick to equipment to identify their calibration status along with due date. Measuring and test equipment is handled, preserved, stored and safeguarded from adjustments to preserve its accuracy and fitness for use. When measuring and test equipment is found to be out of tolerance/ calibration, an assessment of the validity of previous measurements of effected products is assessed and action will be taken as required. Operating Procedure, Control of Monitoring and Measuring Equipment, regulates all activities associated with the monitoring, control and calibration of measuring and test equipment.

7. **Communication:** Management shall formulate communication protocol to the organization regarding the effectiveness of the Quality Management System. Communication is provided by

- Planning meetings,
- Tool box talk & Safety meetings,
- Management reviews,
- One on one meeting,
- Performance reviews,
- Resource group meeting

8. **Documentation process**: This forms very important part of any quality system and shall include information required by the ISO 9000-2015 Standard and documented information determined to be required for the effective operation of the company.

Documents required for the Quality Management System are controlled;

Processes have been established and implemented for maintenance of documents and data as described in standard Operating Procedure, Control of Documents.

- Approving documents for adequacy prior to issue;
- Reviewing, updating when necessary, and re-approving, by the same function, such

documents, and identify revisions;

- Ensuring that relevant versions of applicable documents are available at point of use;
- Ensuring that documents remain legible, readily identifiable and retrievable;
- Preventing the unintended use of obsolete documents and their retention period, and maintain suitable identification if they are retained; and
- A master index will be maintained to identify current revision of all procedures.

Documents and document changes may be initiated by anyone in the organization but may only be issued by an authorized department manager as defined in Operating Procedure, Quality System Documentation, and Operating Procedure, Control of Documents. All documents are reviewed and approved prior to issue. Documents and data are distributed to personnel and locations where they are used. When appropriate and relevant, a distribution list is maintained. Document placement is regulated. Document changes are reviewed and authorized by the same authority that issued the original document. Customer design changes and modifications are processed per the Contract Review Procedures. Engineering Team reviews and approves the changes, and processes any changes required in existing documentation. Revised portions of documents are distributed with a change brief, and obsolete documents are removed. A Master List is maintained specifying the latest issues and revisions of its' documents. At a minimum, documents are subject to review during internal auditing. Documents will be updated as required and re-approved by the issuing authority. Obsolete documents retained for legal and/ or knowledge preservation purposes are suitably identified.

Controls relevant to Documented Information (Records) required for the Quality Management System are established and implemented for maintenance of documents and data as described in Operating Procedure, Record Control.

- Record control is established, implemented and maintained for storage, protection, retrieval, retention period, and disposal as defined in Operating Procedure, Record Control, of the records.

- The records shall be identifiable to the product or process involved.

- When required documents of external origin will be controlled.

- They shall be stored in facilities that provide a suitable environment to minimize deterioration or damage and to prevent loss.

- Records are to be maintained and retained as defined in the record index or as specified by applicable industry

II. ISO 55000 for Asset Management

Asset management is about coordinating and optimizing the management of an asset across its whole lifecycle, including selection, acquisition, development, maintenance, renewal and disposal processes.

ISO 55000 comprises three standards for asset management, namely:

- ISO 55000, which illustrates the scope and merits of asset management while also introducing terms and definitions of the standard;

- ISO 55001, which specifies requirements for integrated and effective asset management systems, similar to the way ISO 9001 specifies quality management requirements.

- ISO 55002, which provides implementation guidelines for asset management systems that adhere to previous standards of the ISO 55000 family.

ISO 55000 contains seven areas of compliance (As per the publically available table of contents):

CONTEXT OF THE ORGANISATION	• Organisational Objectives. • Stakeholders requirements • Asset management system scope • Asset management strategy
LEADERSHIP	• Leadership commitment • Asset Management • Roles, Responsibilities & Authorities
PLANNING	• Risk & Opportunity

SUPPORT	• Resources • Competence • Awareness • Information requirements • Documentation
OPERATION	• Planning, Implementation & control. • Management of change. • Outsourcing
PERFORMANCE EVALUATION	• Monitoring, Measurement, Analysis & Evaluation. • Internal Audit • Management Review
IMPROVEMENT	• Nonconformity & corrective action. • Preventive action • Continual Improvement

In addition to outlining asset management processes and their implementation, ISO 55000 provides in practice a framework for auditing existing asset management implementations in terms of completeness, while also suggesting improvements to existing processes.

Adopting ISO 55000 will allow organization to align the way assets are managed and maintained, it improves return on investments by reducing costs, while supporting asset value without sacrificing organizational objectives.

III. ANSI TAPPI TIP 0305-34:2008

This standard is specified as part of Technical Information Paper TIP 0305-34 and provides guidelines for creating maintenance checklists on a daily, weekly or monthly basis.

In practice, maintenance engineers and users are expected to customize these checklists to the needs of their plant taking into account machines, equipment, physical configurations and other characteristics of the plant.

Documented research efforts and industrial case studies have underlined the importance of maintenance checklists towards focused and effective maintenance. The TAPPI TIP 0305-34:2008 standard provides a practical approach on how to compile and maintain a relevant checklist.

IV. ISO – 50001 Energy Management System

An energy management system helps organizations better manage their energy use, thus improving productivity. It involves developing and implementing an energy policy, setting achievable targets for energy use, and designing action plans to reach them and measure progress. This might include implementing new energy-efficient technologies, reducing energy waste or improving current processes to cut energy costs. ISO 50001 gives organizations a recognized

ISO 50001 gives organizations a recognized framework for developing an effective energy management system. Like other ISO management system standards, it follows the "Plan-Do-Check-Act" process for continual improvement. ISO 50001 provides a set of requirements that enable organizations to:

- Develop a policy for more efficient use of energy
- Fix targets and objectives to meet that policy
- Gather data to better understand and make decisions concerning energy use
- Measure the results obtained
- Review the effectiveness of the policy
- Continually improve energy management

V. ISO-45001 – Occupational Health and Safety Managements Systems

ISO 45001:2018 specifies requirements for an occupational health and safety (OH&S) management system, and gives guidance for its use, to enable organizations to provide safe and healthy workplaces by preventing work-related injury and ill health, as well as by proactively improving its OH&S performance.

ISO 45001:2018 is applicable to any organization that wishes to establish, implement and maintain an OH&S management system to improve occupational health and safety, eliminate hazards and minimize OH&S risks (including system deficiencies), take advantage of OH&S

opportunities, and address OH&S management system nonconformities associated with its activities.

ISO 45001:2018 helps an organization to achieve the intended outcomes of its OH&S management system. Consistent with the organization's OH&S policy, the intended outcomes of an OH&S management system include:

a. continual improvement of OH&S performance;

b. fulfilment of legal requirements and other requirements;

c. achievement of OH&S objectives.

ISO 45001:2018 is applicable to any organization regardless of its size, type and activities. It is applicable to the OH&S risks under the organization's control, taking into account factors such as the context in which the organization operates and the needs and expectations of its workers and other interested parties.

ISO 45001:2018 does not state specific criteria for OH&S performance, nor is it prescriptive about the design of an OH&S management system.

ISO 45001:2018 enables an organization, through its OH&S management system, to integrate other aspects of health and safety, such as worker wellness/wellbeing.

ISO 45001:2018 does not address issues such as product safety, property damage or environmental impacts, beyond the risks to workers and other relevant interested parties.

ISO 45001:2018 can be used in whole or in part to systematically improve occupational health and safety management. However, claims of conformity to this document are not acceptable unless all its requirements are incorporated into an organization's OH&S management system and fulfilled without exclusion.

VI. ISO 14001 – Environmental Management System

International standard ISO 14001 has helped many companies to improve their Environmental Management System (EMS). The operational control element of ISO 14001 ensures that organizations plan such maintenance and carry it out under controlled conditions. Another element of the standard requires the organization to maintain records to demonstrate that it meets the requirements of its EMS. Maintenance activities subject to operational control would fall in this category. The EMS could be integrating in the Quality Management System (QMS) which was certified by ISO 9002.

The environmental policy includes a commitment of compliance with the legislation in force. The key activities are:

- repair, rehabilitation and modernization of the equipment owned;
- get out of operation the obsolete and polluting equipment (for example, electric capacitor types
- which contains synthetic oil with PCB exceed the admitted limits);
- design and build new substations at international standard level;
- take specific actions to mitigate the substations impact upon the environment;
- develop ecologically oriented training for operator

The environmental policy includes a commitment of compliance with the legislation in force. The key activities are:

- Repair, rehabilitation and modernization of the equipment owned;
- get out of operation the obsolete and polluting equipment (for example, electric capacitor types which contains synthetic oil with PCB exceed the admitted limits);
- design and build new substations at international standard level;
- take specific actions to mitigate the substations impact upon the environment;
- develop ecologically oriented training for operator

ISO 14001 Procedure –

- Identify the environmental aspects and assess the significant impacts of the Plant equipment on environment.

- Identify and record the environmental regulations and other requirements (in order to obtain environmental permits)

- Set the environmental objectives and targets.

- Set the organizational structure, assignments and responsibilities for implementation of EHS.

- Organize specific training for employees (related to environmental aspects)

- Develop EMS documents and control

- Operational control

- Emergency preparedness (incidents, accidents) and response

- Monitor and measure the activities with significant negative impact upon the environment.

- Identification, analysis and working on nonconformities, corrective and preventive action.

- Issuing, filing and eliminating the environmental records

- EMS audit and EMS review performed by the management

Potentially, equipment that is referenced in the EMS will include any item whose failure or improper operation or repair may result in release of hazardous or toxic materials into the environment. This may be a significant number of equipment items.

Companies operating in a reactive management mode may see the cost associated with such failures as an opportunity to establish a toehold on moving toward the preventive, predictive, or productive modes. Such a strategy can address two problems simultaneously. First, since reactive organizations are most likely to be responsible for environmental aspects, exposure to environmental penalties can be reduced. Second, operational efficiency can improve due less unplanned downtime. Companies implementing EMS will address specific attention to:

- Preventive Maintenance (PM) programs and activities;

- Predictive Maintenance (Pd M) programs and activities;

- Maintenance planning, scheduling and backlog management;
- Additional tracking in the computerized maintenance management system (CMMS);
- Root cause analysis (RCA) procedures and records.

Although these changes in maintenance practices may seem time-consuming at first, they don't all need to be implemented at once.

1. Preventive Maintenance (PM) programs and activities. PM is planned maintenance of substation and equipment that is designed to improve equipment life and avoid any unplanned maintenance activity. PM includes painting, lubrication, cleaning, adjusting and minor component replacement to extend the life of equipment and facilities. Analysis and optimization of the PM program for equipment items associated with the organization's significant environmental aspects will be necessary to make sure that maintenance is adequately planned. This could provide the stimulus to have a detailed look into the PM program and its coverage.

   How are potentially significant environmental impacts addressed in the substation and plants for PM activities?

   - Examine existing PM activities as they come due and modify them to take into account the analysis of environmental aspects as directed by ISO 14002.

   - Begin with a list of the organization's significant environmental aspects, check for appropriate PM coverage, and set up PM actions as needed.

2. Predictive Maintenance (PdM) programs and activities. In many substations, maintenance service is based on some reading measurement going beyond the predetermined limit. In Pd M, the equipment is inspected and based on the condition, further work or inspection are done. This means that the type and frequency of maintenance will be dictated by the ability of the equipment to produce the outputs required, i.e.its condition. Condition

monitoring tasks include actions such as visual inspection or other sophisticated technologies. At the top of the list of technologies are the latest techniques in line-one monitoring and expert diagnostics. In order to do this, the condition of the item of equipment or critical components of the equipment must be measured.

There are various techniques available and measurements must be made at regular intervals and trends analyzed. Examining the trends and with a knowledge of the failure characteristics of the items, enable preventive or corrective maintenance work to be planned and applied without risk of failure of the items to perform their duties. The successful applications of PdM techniques leads to fewer planned and unplanned plant stoppages, lower maintenance man-hours and reduced expenditure on spare parts.

PdM actions (vibration monitoring, oil analysis, thermal imaging, predictive electrical testing, power supply monitoring, materials thickness testing, predictive electrical testing, ultrasonic inspection, visual inspection) are focused on more critical equipment and this proactive approach may be suited for equipment associated with the organization's significant environmental aspects.

How are these records kept and how can they be used to demonstrate proactive compliance with EMS?

• Looking into PdM program can take the same two starting points as in the PM program above.

3. Maintenance planning, scheduling and backlog management. More maintenance work is accomplished in less time using the same resources than would be the case if the planning function did not exist.

If the bottom line is not improved by having a planning function, it is usually the result of poorly defined roles and responsibilities, an absence of understanding of the planning role and its value, a lack of support from management, insufficient planner training, or having the wrong people in the planning role.

Backlog is the list of work generated as work order requests. Backlog management is an important tool for determining maintenance department resource, making budget and workforce staffing decisions, evaluating department performance and analyzing alternatives. Taking advantage of opportunities created by job planning requires coordination and cooperation of production and maintenance to use job planning in ways that actually reduce the time it takes to complete each job.

What Key Performance Indicators are in place for assessing whether the organization is complying with its operational controls and achieving its objectives for environmental performance?

- Substation Surface (m2), Oil amounts in Equipment (tones), SF6 in Equipment (kg), PCB Power Capacitors (pieces), Noise Level (dB), Electrical Field (kV/cm), Reused Wastes (tones) etc.

4. Additional tracking in the computerized maintenance management system (CMMS). The CMMS is a great tool for tracking environmental compliance. Adding an equipment classification for those items associated with significant aspects is in obvious change to make. There maywell be new equipment items to include in the hierarchy.

- It is possible to display and print a list of equipment that is covered under the EMS.

- EHS may even use the CMMS as its basic environmental data tool.

5. Root cause analysis (RCA) procedures and records. In event there are environmental aspects, the root cause analysis procedures, operational control procedures, and record keeping will be scrutinized for their effectiveness in finding and eliminating the source of excursions not only for the specific incident, but extended

to all such similar actions and equipment items in the plant. In fact, the EMS will require that specific RCA procedure be established, implemented and maintained.ISO 14001 represents a social move toward greater organizational responsibility in protecting and restoring our planet's resources and support systems. It is up to private and public companies to make internal changes to reduce their negative impact. Realizing environmental protection is just plain good business, and profitable for all, too.

Other Plant Specific Process – In addition to above there are some other industry specific process as implemented across industries are to be complied with standards i.e., as Good Manufacturing practices in Pharmaceutical sector, TPM applicable in most of automobile industries etc

In addition to standard process industries may use quality initiatives as autonomous maintenance, Six sigmas' etc. However, these process is driven by Industry specific Manufacturing unit& plants. Service partners in business are expected to be conversant with these processes along with its direct and indirect benefit known to each employee, to ensure effectiveness of these programs can be in multiple folds.

VIEWPOINT

- Manufacturing organisation sometimes outsource there specialised core manufacturing function, which distinguish them from competitors for commanding premium on services.

- Outsourcing maintenance services can be compared with Gymnasium, Yoga or meditation centre, with competant trainer to guide for maintaining good health. In case of any issues identified at early stage i.e. any discomfort on trade mill may indicate cardiac or any other health issue for which specialist at hospital can be consulted.

Chapter 2

Models and Philosophies

"Do what you do best, and outsource the rest."

– Peter Drucker

The maintenance outsourcing emerged as need of time, when initially high technology capital equipment sold in the market with very little know how available in public domain. The customer in such cases, proposes to take up the O & M of equipment as a condition to purchase the equipment. Later OEM agreed and O&M become successful model with regular cash flow and attractive proposition.

The outsourcing services are usually considered and sold in market as service support for non-core activities and is categorized differently by different industries. To be precise in any business main objective is profitability & all other activities can be considered as non-core activities. This broad classification can be summarized as with some outsourcing as in practice in Industries:

Earning Decent Profit – Final Objectives (Common for any Service provider or Industry unit)

Sales & Business Development – In house, although part of marketing including digital marketing can be outsourced.

Business Administration – In house (Usually carried out by owner)

Logistic – Variable part like transportation of staff, Trucks for material transport and Earthmover heavy equipment's services are provided by contractors.

Quality control – This generally, remains to be in house activity.

Manufacturing – In some business like API and few other categories complete manufacturing at different times has been outsourced. i.e. operation and maintenance of power plant are also outsourced activities.

Product development/improvement – Usually it is in house and rarely a candidate for outsourcing.

Asset maintenance & Management – These services can be outsourced to different local contractors& established players. AMC of special/critical equipment also falls in the same category.

Supply chain management – Usually done by owner, some part in different proportion can be outsourced.

Human resources – Recruitment activity can be outsourced; Variable manpower can be provided by local contractors.

Others (Security, Catering, Housekeeping, gardening etc.) – Services usually outsourced

All above listed functions are component of any normal operating Industry. Different factors like Product complexity, Market etc. forms criteria for outsourcing or not. Here we will limit to only maintenance outsourcing within the scope of this book.

Outsourcing Models in Practice – Outsourcing is complex feature as directly affecting cost and quality of service with involvement of all departments of manufacturing unit needs substantial focus in terms of models.

The outsourcing models can be broadly classified based on scope as –

i. Preventive maintenance model-

- Service provider here being responsible for fixed PM with associated fixed fees.

- Normally includes some corrective elements i.e. filter cleaning.

- Any repair or reactive work is excluded or carried out at unit rate i.e. cable laying at Rs./mtr.

- Major risk lies with asset owner.

- Requirement not being clear, no scientific methodology of maintenance leads to anywhere between excess maintenance to minimum maintenance depending upon mutual consent.
- Budgeting and cost control is not very effective.

ii. Inspection/Audits (or reactive) based-

- Site Inspection/Audits conducted by team deployed.
- Usually fixed inspection fees.
- Not includes any repair or reactive work. Excludes any corrective element i.e. filter cleaning.
- Scope includes only recommendations and reporting issues.
- Least cost with minimal effectiveness.

iii. End result/(Reliability based) Model-

- Trend of present times.
- Partial risk shared by service provider. Risk based on defined end result requirement (e.g. Fuel efficiency, comfort etc.)
- Payment based on results. i.e. linked with KPI or productivity.
- Usually tied to guaranteed maximum price(GMP). Proportionate deduction assigned on non achievement of agreed performance.
- Difficulty in deciding mutually agreeable defined parameters.

iv. Comprehensive-

- This model comprise of fixed fees with all material, spares & materials inclusive.
- Major risk lies with contractor.
- Excludes capital replacement, refurbishment and/or rehabilitation.
- Usually subject to condition assessment and latent condition.

- Contractor has to establish balance between reduced risk high reliability within planned budget.
- Significant administration cost saving for client.

v. Semi-comprehensive-

- Includes of all expert and labour cost only.
- Fixed labour fees.
- Normally excludes parts and materials.
- Optimum for large sites/Portfolios.
- Risk lies with Asset owner.
- Budget is simple and provision is provided in Asset management.

vi. Repair work limit-

- This mostly includes services like modernisation, refurbishment, Major overhaul etc.
- Most reactive calls are included.
- Capped risk at predetermined/agreed threshold on RWL.
- Usually subject to condition assessment and latent condition.
- Signification administration saving for client.

Above are the some of the common models of outsourcing and many more flexible models with best of different combinations can be worked out as per customer specific requirement and services incorporated in contract.

Too frequently, the industry's clients have been excited about commitments, but disappointed by the services actually delivered, resulting into customer un-satisfaction and may look for order review or renewal because of system inertia and the cost of change.

In current times, as communication and information technologies have become more prominent, service solutions have continued to evolve, and with interoperability the norm, outsourcing outcomes have been able to be different. This is probably the time to move away from integrated service

(Single window) delivery through a single managing contractor to considering 'best of expert class' solutions, all interlinked through a service integrator.

Above all it also needs to have serious thought towards expert services requirement and its extent, under which function as cost still remains the most important factor in current time to remain competitive in market place. i.e. Earlier reliability was the major issue with heavy machine and complex engineering. Due to limited access of public to technology, expertise is the monopoly with OEM because of their facility set up with large capital and competent team of service engineers.

With change in time and developed technology the major capital-intensive plant machinery and equipment has become more reliable and trustworthy on mechanical front, alongside peripheral automation i.e. PLC, IOT, AI, Machine learning occupying central stage with multiple vendors in market place and best ground for technology upgrade with overall system effectiveness.

Service Level Inconsistencies

In the past, there has been significant effort invested in structuring integrated service delivery platforms that could provide consistent levels of service standards across very different types of service categories in different industries, each having their own challenges.

Through experience across various industry portfolios serviced in outsourced contracts, it has become evident that human behaviours, competency requirement vary across the different industries within different sectors.

For example "Factors that motivate and forms key for an industry in auto sector may be vastly different to those that motivate an industry in metal or cement sector". Yet across many integrated service delivery platforms, these differences are not recognised in structuring the performance management frameworks.

By persisting with integrated service delivery platforms across various industries, facilities and projects with prescriptive and onerous performance management frameworks, based on similarly structured service performance standards, it is likely that the contracts are being set up to fail and has been evident in a number of contracts.

The reality is that the approach to Industry service performance across disciplines and functions is best-measured using methods closely aligned to each. This is also true across geographies. Although it may be an enviable aspiration to have one enterprise, and one standard approach, this neglects cultural and regional differences and capabilities.

Expert Services by Specialist Contractors

More and more client organisations are moving to models where it is possible to procure 'best of specialist (Expert)' service contractors for specific functions and regions.

Although most management contract models are structured to have the client participate in the procurement process to achieve this kind of outcome, this seldom provides the level of flexibility and control needed.

The contract governance structure and the performance management framework usually mean that 'interference' by the client is not an ideal condition to be in and once these forms of client input start to occur, the management contractor may take the approach of stepping aside to abdicate decisions and accountability to the client. This is not an ideal way either to administer a management contract with a fee attached.

At the same time, service providers are moving to providing significant components of direct delivery for specialist services because of reducing industry margins. Direct delivery capacity building in specialist areas within the large service providers is becoming the industry norm. In addition, trade purchases in the industry, with larger companies buying up the smaller specialist service providers, is unlikely to go away soon.

This new trend goes some way to eliminating the 'margin on margin' debate around management contractors procuring and managing a wide range of specialist subcontractors for a fee or additional cost layer. However, with this trend occurring, access to best of expert subcontractors is less likely to be accommodated within integrated service delivery contract structures.

Therefore, access to 'best of expert' specialist service providers, both related to particular services and local geographies, will likely need an alternative contract structure.

This is particularly relevant for clients who accept that Industrial services and facilities management is not part of their core business and the management of multiple service providers, as well as the overlay of the required portfolio data and information, should be outsourced.

Basic Industrial firm's motivation and marketing strategy of service provider being an increased focus on core activities and reduced ownership of non-core activities. Classifying activities into core and non-core activities is also difficult task and broadly classified as close associate and distant associate in manufacturing process. Since maintenance is a support function strongly linked to the production core in a manufacturing firm. Governing maintenance outsourcing relies on the interdependencies between maintenance and core production. The equipment performance in process industries (such as aluminum & cement industry) is critical, and effective maintenance is crucial for competitiveness as well as increased maintenance cost or equipment failure effect business bottom line.

Process industry plants are complex systems with many interlinked activities, distinguishing of activity as core and noncore is difficult.

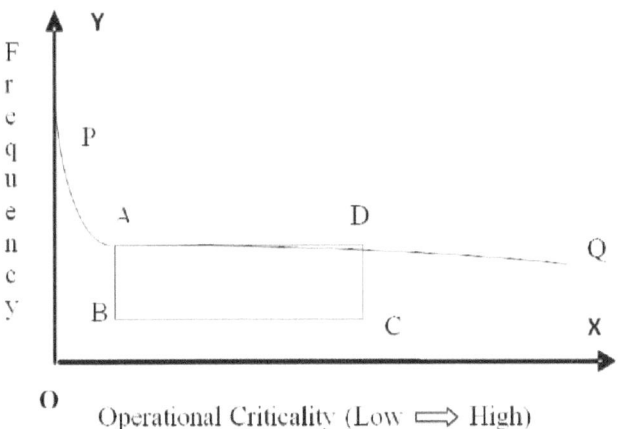

Fig – II

The Probability/criticality curve Fig-II, here shows area "PA" and "DQ" candidate for outsourcing, although for different reasons and have different eligibility criteria. "PA" being low skill area can be managed by anylocal/general service provider at considerably lower price. "DQ" is high skill and specialized resource intensive activity and outsourced due to its specialization characteristic. Here when we say Specializations, which usually means extensive process specialization, moreover not limited to general component, level i.e. Motors, Valves etc.

The region in rectangle ABCD is the area where maximum part of manufacturing operation falls with scope of cost optimization and value addition. This region of maintenance can be carried out in house or outsourced to service provider at either side of the curve.

When operator in region "PA" extends service under the region AB quality is a concern and need to be closely supervised. On contrary specialized service provider of region DQ are expensive enough on account of associated overhead cost. It's the role of SCM and engineering team in organization to work out the best optimum solution for their industrial unit.

It's similar to any good hospital, where patient wards are classified as general ward & different special wards with premium pricing depending upon the ward facilities. In such hospitals premium is charged wardwise, categorized as ICU, General ward, Special ward & Special ward with twin sharing etc. In such hospitals premium is also charged on other services like Doctor visit charge, ECG etc. Irrespective of being at par in all wards. It means same Doctor visiting different wards are charged differently. That means premium charged on similar services as package deal on opting for premium ward.

Maintenance must be seen as a supply chain of its own. That's because production plant maintenance is not directly involved in the supply chain of firms 'core production but rather supports the core supply chain, in other words the production line, with corrective and preventive maintenance services.

Governance structures and mechanisms must allow for flexible adaptation to changing circumstances and uncertainty in the downstream relationships. Management to work out strategy and assign coordinator to deal with control problems in interfirm relationships by selecting an appropriate partner. Furthermore, the partner selection phase influences both collaboration and the use of governance arrangements.

Refer Fig. III below Quadrant 1 (Q1) is the category of suppliers with relatively low technical and organizational capabilities, sourced by traditional arm's-length contracts, often as sub-suppliers at planned shut-downs. They possess neither the organizational capability needed for relational forms of collaboration nor the technical skill to do strategically important core-close maintenance. In quadrant 2, highly mature suppliers can be expected. The low technical capability could indicate entrance in a new market; therefore, the potential to leverage the position into quadrant 4 is very high. Until then, they are governed with market contracts based on price, mostly for corrective maintenance. In quadrant 3, modular contractors making services or products such as spare parts to customer's specifications could be expected when the suppliers increase their maturity close to the client Vision level. In quadrant 4 are found the suppliers with capability to manage deep collaboration and partnerships. They also have the technical skills to perform core-close maintenance, both corrective and preventive, as well as to develop more competitive maintenance process.

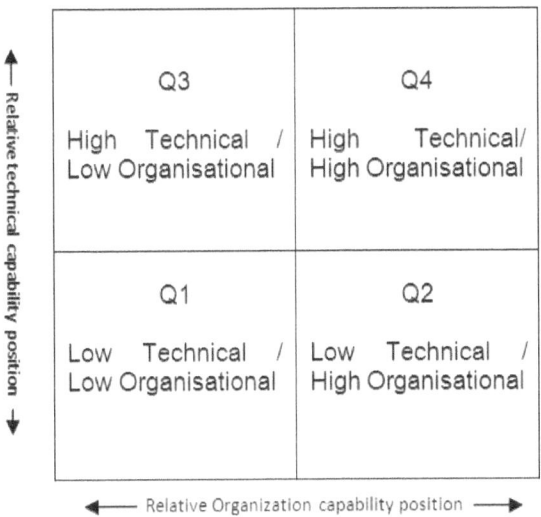

Fig.-III

Maintenance Types and Methods

The maintenance process is performed as follows: When a problem is detected, it is necessary to determine its cause, so that it can be quickly corrected or re installed. There are many methods and types of maintenance. The following represents most of them:

- Run-to-failure: This method is suitable for minor corrective work, low price equipment and components.

- Corrective maintenance: This is done after a failure, to restore an item to a state in which it can perform its required function.

- Scheduled maintenance: Periodic inspection of facilities, carry out schedule maintenance and replacement of components.

- Planned maintenance: This is carried out with foresight, control and the use of records to a predetermined plan.

- Preventive maintenance: This keeps a facility operating efficiently through regular inspection, and it aims to tackle small problems before they become expensive.

- Condition-based maintenance: If maintenance is based on expected failure of the component, it includes scheduled and corrective maintenance.

- Predictive condition monitoring: This is performed by the application of multiple technologies to monitor the condition of items.

- Reliability-centered maintenance: This method is used to determine the maintenance requirements of any asset in its operating context, and to improve the asset promptly instead of rectifying it in the future.

- Total productive maintenance: This includes many methods to improve reliability, quality, and production. By combining with the effort of operators for safety, and quality.

- Proactive maintenance: This reduces the total maintenance required through advanced performance including preventive/predictive maintenance.

- Maintenance management metric: This allocates the value-added resources for improving component's overall effectiveness, and optimizing the cost per unit of production.

- Total quality maintenance: Total quality maintenance is a method for monitoring and controlling deviations in a service's quality by detecting and preventing the causes of failure. By this a strategy, the user maintains the technical and economic effectiveness of the process elements.

Maintenance Strategies

Organisations are faced daily with difficult strategic decisions on how to invest in an efficient and effective way in their plant maintenance regimes. For many, yearly budgets for maintenance are not large enough to cover all desired works, so it is essential that maintenance measures meet statutory legislative requirements.

An organisation's sustainability can be threatened if the minimum requirements at least are not met. The consequences of not doing so include:

- increased risk to people's health and safety
- the potential for legal enforcement
- significant consequences to service operations
- lower staff morale
- the escalation of capital needed due to increased running costs.

Traditionally, actions are prioritised first by considering statutory and occupational health and safety requirements followed closely by business critical and operational requirements, with the remainder of issues with a lesser impact pushed back to a later time when resources are available.

Statutory obligations do tend to consume a large portion of budgets. However, insufficient investment can lead to postponement of key major repairs and replacements, creating backlogs which can lead to ad hoc critical works being done at a higher cost. If the assets do fall below minimum standards and possibly beyond economical repair, this could lead to having to replace them altogether.

A risk-based methodology can help decisions when planning maintenance programmes, allowing responsible members from both side i.e. Client and service provider to prioritise the works deemed of high or significant risk while considering ongoing daily maintenance requirements to prevent the assets from falling into disrepair.

Types of Maintenance

The types of maintenance that organisations are likely to be faced with can be broadly divided into "reactive" or "planned" categories.

Reactive maintenance: also known as "corrective" maintenance refers to often costly ad hoc interventions to respond to a failure. These could be identified either by general observations or incidents during day-to-day functioning. They can be:

- routine repairs of any minor breakages with limited impact
- urgent repairs required to minimise any disruption due to unforeseen breakdown
- emergency repairs due to imminent risks to health and safety, or cause of major disruptions.

Most reactive works generally cannot be deferred, although certain non-serious repairs can be grouped together then become part of the planned maintenance if they do not pose a significant risk.

Planned maintenance also known as "preventive" or "lifecycle" maintenance, is a cost effective and efficient way of planning future maintenance works. These can either be identified by periodic statutory inspections as required by legislation, where corrective actions are identified for a equipment to remain compliant, or works forming lifecycle maintenance, identified through Equipment condition monitoring/Test reports which highlight works needed to extend the life of an asset. This process is a way of forward planning which aims to avoid any breakdowns and to maintain the integrity of the fabric of the plant machinery and ensures that it operates at its maximum efficiency. Depending on an organisation's asset strategy and risk appetite, these works are then grouped and prioritised into:

- essential works
- important works
- desirable works.

Any maintenance works deferred due to lack of funds or any other reasons form the backlog. These need to be reviewed and considered whenever future planned programmes are reviewed with the aim to reduce the backlog over time. Otherwise, these jobs become a liability and could cause an unwanted event or become beyond economical repair.

Maintenance Management Approach (Risk Based)

A risk-based approach allows organisations to evaluate the criticality and the consequence of potential failures against the likelihood of the event happening. These scores are ranked and works can be prioritised according to the severity of the risk. This focuses on the key risks while not ignoring day-to-day affairs. The approach combines asset information with engineering knowledge and practical experience, in order to make a balanced decision on priorities. The organisation's degree of risk appetite can also be taken into account when asking the important questions.

- What degree of work being deferred is acceptable?
- What level of risk is acceptable?
- What is the life expectancy of the asset?

The process is as follows.

- First, identify the risk and the severity of the impact should a failure occur, relating to the physical condition or the compliance required. Risks can be considered as being strategic (where failure would have a negative impact on an organization's objective) or operational (where there are impacts to daily operations).

- Next, categorise the risks in terms of the likelihood of the undesirable event happening. The estimation should be based on previous historical information and competent technical judgment.

- The level of risk can then be calculated for each item or scenario by multiplying the level of impact of the failure by the likelihood or probability of the failure happening.

- The level of risk then is used to assess which pose the greatest level of threat to the organisation. This creates the priority list.

Low-risk essentials that fully comply with current statutory requirements can have works done at a later date.

Medium-risk essentials that comply fully with statutory requirements but require only minor actions of non-serious nature can be dealt with by close monitoring and included in maintenance programmes.

Significant risk elements, and where there is a breach of legislation, require action in the short term and need to be prioritised.

High-risk elements and those that seriously breach legislation require immediate attention to prevent catastrophic events.

Don't risk it!

The condition of assets are constantly changing and, if left unattended, will deteriorate. Having a risk-based approach for decision-making with regards to maintenance helps to optimise the efficiency of that maintenance.

Maintenance Outsourcing – Team Philosophy at Work

One of the most important aspects in outsourcing, when services are extended to wide range of industries and customers with different priorities and approach. Lot in these businesses depends upon relationship management and synergy.

First, let's define work. It is the same word as energy. En-ergia means to be at work. The very heart of work is energy, the same $E=mc^2$. Without it, nothing gets done. We also need intelligence to guide work. What is intelligence? Intelligence has multiple meanings, as Luke Muehlhauser who defined it in his book, Facing the Intelligence Explosion. Intelligence means the efficient and optimized domination of multiple environments. Intelligence is what gives humans their advantage over competitors.

We can argue that another name for thinking or philosophy is ultimately about the systemized use of intelligence or, in other words, about winning customer. In order to win you must deploy knowledge or systemic rationality. This is the craft of obtaining true beliefs. We continually are able to update our beliefs using logic, probability theory and decision making theory. Finally, we act for the sake of our goals. As Aristotle teaches, our ultimate goal is happiness, which is achieved by living the good life. Does all this begin to sound like the stuff that drives business leaders?

The key to successful business today is innovation and the ability to ride the wave of accelerating technological evolution. Only lean startup companies seem able to move with the necessary speed to bring innovation and disruptive technologies to the table to satisfy an ever-hungrier customer base clamoring for the latest innovations.

How will traditional companies survive in such an environment? I argue that only through philosophy will this be possible. Only philosophy offers the opportunity to make the necessary culture changes that will foster innovation within an organization. As Peter Drucker, the well-known management philosopher and guru has said "culture eats strategy for lunch."

So how does a large corporation go about changing its corporate culture to foster innovation? The way forward for such companies requires a transformative process of surfacing and committing to core values. This is an exercise in applied ethics.

When we look at the old hierarchical corporate institution, we can see it in terms of what's called a autocratic culture. Leadership, is characterized by a boss, who implicitly or explicitly says **"I am great and you are not so great"** Working for such a boss demeans workers. In such a culture, there is no energy, enthusiasm, or initiative and, as a result, no possibility of innovation. So how does an organization change its culture to succeed?

An organization must commit to core values and a noble cause through ethical dialogue. A healthy, culture defines itself as **"We are great."** This is a "one for all and all for one" culture. Everyone in it is proud to be a member.

In ancient Greece, no ship would set sail without a seer or visionary aboard who would be able to see and avoid the dangerous shoals the ship might encounter. In the same way, a visionary leader, consultant, or officer in the organization will scan the horizon of the future for the upcoming technologies with cost benefit analysis and advise the organization on a course of risk assessment, alternative scenarios, and innovative developments that will avert corporate disaster.

Industry Specific Outsourcing

Similar industries possess similar culture and maintenance practices. Few of the industrial model for reference are discussed as hereunder:

Power plants – Indian power plant has come across long way from initially complete in house operation & Maintenance to Complete outsourcing model for operation and maintenance. The entire range of Power Plant O & M is split into different stages between two extremes comprising of different proportion of the outsourced services.

The power sector has been more dynamic in last two decades with different technology and cost model updating becoming continuous process right from fossil fuel operated plant based on Heavy fuel/HSD to Thermal plant and even now extending to Solar plants and wind mills.

There are five predominant types of models as followed by IPP and CPP as enlisted hereunder-

1. 100% In house O & M.

2. Maintenance outsourcing only.

3. Basic O & M outsourcing including only day to day operation and minor activities.

4. Enhanced O & M outsourcing including spare management etc.

5. 100% Outsourcing including operation and maintenance, coal/ash handling etc.

Each of these model of O&M comes with their own share of pros and cons. While maintenance outsourcing provides more control to the IPPs, the owner is exposed to other operational risks. The 100% outsourcing model has the possibility to de-risk the IPP/CPP from operational risks, however it comes with high cost adversely affecting the bottom line. Companies decide their strategy based on past experience and risk appetite.

Now a days upcoming practice is that power plants not awarding complete O&M to single party service provider but splitting O & M outsourcing into smaller packages like BTG, CHP,AHP, Electrical & Switchyards. This not only help in reduce risk and dependency on single service provider but also adds into bargaining power for the management.

On the flip side, such model calls for better management and coordination among various contractors and the owners to ensure adherence to service level agreement.

Pharmaceutical API Industries – The outsourcing of utility services within the pharmaceuticals industry in most cases include clean utility system such as high purity water and steam systems(purified water, water for injection, clean steam) and clean room Heating ventilation and Air conditioning (HVAC). Facility services will typically include building fabric maintenance, cleaning and general building service administration.

Outsourcing to right partner with well-established clear objective may lead to great results. Outsourcing doesn't mean to relinquishing of overall responsibility. For example, in pharmaceutical industry, legal aspects such as regulatory compliance for drug manufacturing must be maintained and closely monitored and outsourcing company must provide safe systems of work. Outsourcing of utilities (particularly clean utilities) and facilities should be a risk – based approach where over time, the contract company becomes more empowered through satisfaction by the client company that high quality services can be consistently delivered. Outsourcing partners to have a high degree of ownership when it comes to operating and maintaining utility/facilities systems. Performance is measured through areas, such as availability, planned work vs Actual, safety and regulatory requirements. For clean utility systems, high level compliance is ensured through subject matter experts and quality assurance team of respective section.

Within the outsourcing structure, the internal site training systems should be adopted by the contract company for areas such as procedural, GMP and safety compliance.

Data Centre: Maintenance is crucial to keep critical data center reliable, but any work on live equipment might put the facility at risk. Data centre engineering may split job as which entrust certain hardware to in-house staff, but more complex systems that could cause damages should go to third-party service providers to avoid expensive errors or unexpected downtime.

Every data center is different, and system oriented approach ensure to improve and sustain maintenance process at desired level. Equipment checklists for technicians formatted and revised periodically.System audit and service provider documentation review keeps performance in control. The major utility in Data centre comprise of Cooling system, UPS system, Fire Protection system as critical set up in addition to other general plant utilities.

Other Industries: All other industries like Automobiles, Steel industry, Metal & Mining etc. all are adopting maintenance outsourcing tailored to meet customer requirement.

In addition to improve reliability, efficient operation and cost control the flexibility remains the major advantage of outsourcing. As with in house maintenance, any change or remodel manpower deployment plan will cause dissent and disturbance. In the case of maintenance, outsourcing risk of such variance is borne with service provider. "COVID-19" pandemic is a recent example of it.

VIEWPOINT

- Look into business model of Job placement agency. They provide the resume building services, claiming creating better resume. It is like someone outside in better position to describe you, then you yourself. How relevant is this for Maintenance outsourcing?

Chapter 3

Vendor Evaluation & Cost Validation

"Conformity is the jailer of freedom and the enemy of growth."

– John F Kennedy

Introduction

In selecting a vendor for one or more functions of an entity, management should follow a procedure that includes considerations of key strengths of a vendor the possible risks involved. Vendor strengths mean the benefits that the vendor brings to the operations, their core competencies, and operational capabilities. Risks involved in an outsourcing situation refers to the possibility that the vendor does not live up to the expectations and the outsourcing organization has to deal with the possible consequences. The following generic set of factors have been found to be useful in evaluating vendor strengths. Inherent in each is a consideration of vendor risk. All different vendors/service provider are mapped across different parameters on the industry specific scale. Some parameters can be as:

1. Availability – A vendor should be able to provide uninterrupted service to the Industry (outsourcing establishment). This ability will be dependent on the vendor's operational capabilities and its financial strength.

2. Interest – The selected vendor should have sufficient interest in the functions that are to be outsourced. This interest can be

determined by the subject experience of the vendor, domain expertise, membership in industry organizations, and customer base.

3. Company History-The first and foremost should be a company's record of accomplishment. If the company has been in business for some time, one can get information about that company from industry-specific magazines and trade associations.

4. Industry Organizational members – A vendor's membership in an industry organization lends credibility of operational capability. Any industry organization membership should be looked at as a plus in a vendor's portfolio of competencies.

5. Technology – The vendor should have technologically adequate equipment, facilities and infrastructure to perform the outsourced functions. At the very least, the vendor should have the same or similar technology as the outsourcing firm. If the vendor is unable to provide technologically sound operations, the outsourcing firm will experience lack of quality and performance in the outsourced service.

6. Financial Strength/Stability – Financial strength and stability are important vendor evaluation factors. Such consideration identifies areas of weakness and vendor operational capabilities.

7. Subject Experience Track Record – Besides having strong financial base and a reputable operating history, the company should have adequate and sufficient subject experience. This factor is especially important in the case of industries that require specific licensing to handle jobs. Subject experience can be gauged by reviewing the company's work exposure to like jobs, experience of personnel on like jobs, number of clients being served on similar jobs, and the company's employee turnover rate.

8. Cost – Cost is an important quantitative factor in evaluating and selecting a vendor. The vendor should meet all of the other requisites

and provide the lowest bid. The outsourcing organization should make a cost estimate, and all bids received should be compared to this estimate. This estimate will give the outsourcer a better idea about how realistic a bid is, and will help the outsourcer get a better feel for estimating in the future. The risk associated with accepting a bid based only on cost is present.

9. Quality/Performance – Quality is one of the most important qualitative factors. A complete study should be performed of all quality requirements. Vendor operational efficiency and effectiveness play a significant role in assuring quality of product or service desired. Quality control at the output level should be part of the total quality assurance, which involves operational capabilities. This criteria can be satisfied by professional and industry certification of operations. Quality needs to be assured by the vendor for the life of the contract. The outsourcer needs to make sure that it takes proactive measures to assure consistent quality product or service.

10. Knowledge of the Industry – Vendor knowledge is essential to make sure that the product or service being outsourced is received without disruption. Industry knowledge will help the vendor anticipate peak times of product or service performed and will help the vendor plan for such times.

11. Scope of Service – Scope of service should be defined to the vendor at the outset. Specifically, scope of service should be clearly spelled out in the call for bids. The vendor's industry and subject experience will determine the scope of services that the vendor firm can be realistically expected to perform.

12. Support availability – A vendor should be able to provide as-needed and when-needed service support. If operations are 24 x7, for example, then the support service should also

be available for all function-critical operations. A vendor with support personnel and parts (storage) near the area of operations should be preferred.

13. Backup/Contingency Planning at Site – A vendor should have adequate backup personnel and facilities in case of a natural or human-induced disaster. This capability will ensure non disruptive availability of service. Any unforeseen calamity should result in minimal delays of operations. The loss of production facility by the vendor can lead to total disruption of supply to the outsourcing company.

14. Facilities – A vendor's facilities should be physically and functionally adequate and reasonable. All facilities should be certified by all of the relevant agencies (fire marshal, Motor workshop, Test facility, etc.). All facilities should also have good security measures. Inadequate facilities may lead to closure of such facilities by the regulatory agencies.

15. Contract Adjustments – A vendor should be reasonable as to contract adjustments. In case of unforeseen circumstances, such as obsolescence or abnormality, the outsourcing firm should be able to adjust the contract to better function in such times.

16. Audit/Quality Review – A vendor should have independent review or audit of its operations. This review can be a financial audit/review and a review of operations such as a quality review (ISO etc.). Non-audited or non reviewed operations can lead to doubts about reliability of the operational and financial capability of the vendor.

Regression Technique for Maintenance Contract Pricing

Regression analysis is simply a statistical process that can be used in establishing and predicting the relationship between two or more independent input variables impacting a final dependent output.

Multiple regression model: It is a model that solves and predicts the relationship between variables as Y=a + bX1 + cX2 +dX3, where "Y" is the dependent variable (quoted price) to be correctly predicted, "a" is the intercept or can be considered as constant/fixed cost (defined by the model), "b, c and d" are the slopes/coefficients/sensitivities (also defined by the model) and X1, X2 and X3 are the independent input variables.

Wide combination of linear and logical regression can be employed in deriving the operation cost from both owner and service provider perspective, Although dependent variable (Quote/estimated Price) can be same for both but independent input variables may vary accordingly depending upon priorities and prevalent practices.

The type of industry, Location, KPI, Manpower attrition rate, Expertise/External support requirement etc. can be typical input variables. Data can be collected either on time series basis for same service contract for different period or cross-sectional data for different service contract during same period.

Thereafter scatter chart can be plotted giving indicative price to confirm the deviation from quoted price and revalidate for correctness or accommodate any missed out environmental condition change to avoid the error. As all regression model has life and changes with changing environmental condition.

Let's simplify this by using an example. Let's assume the prices "Y" quoted by different service provider for maintenance contract and is a function of X1 (KPI), X2 (Outside expert service) and X3 (Competency requirement) for different contractors. Simply put, when a regression of this data is run, the negotiator would be able to use the solution to:

o   Test the logic behind the supplier's pricing/quotation;

o   Determine the correct prices (that should be paid) in comparison with the initial supplier quotes;

o   Identify the correct levers to concentrate valuable resources to optimise negotiation result;

o Predict the costs of new activities to be added within the scope, if required;

o Determine the expected change in future budget if any of the independent variables change; and

o Determine the marginal rate of technical substitution of the independent variables.

Regression analysis can be used to study the cost, sourcing complexity, contract price variability for comparing quotation etc. for different contractors.

Cost: Comparing structured vs non structured cost visibility, Unforeseen vs. anticipated expenses are few example for cost.

Complexity: Consider tender situations such as off-the-shelve items Vs customized solution, simple Vs network solutions, KPI attainable by default vs challenging KPI and competitive Vs oligopoly/monopolistic negotiation situations.

Contract price variability: Here consider contract duration and the stability of economic environment. Short term contracts established in a stable economic environment are easier to negotiate but are slightly expensive.

Application of Regression Tool

o It can used with or without benchmark data.

o Where benchmark data is available, it can be considered as the predicted data and negotiate with supplier based on the "line of best fit"

o Where benchmark data is not available, use some agreed logical principle to determine the target rate. Use this target rate to determine the line of best fit. This can then be used to compare with supplier quotation

o Where only the supplier data is available, the negotiator can use regression to test the suppliers pricing logic and to determine the best levers for negotiation. This approach is particularly beneficial as it may make/help the supplier start understanding patterns in his cost model.

o   Use this tool in contracting when owner is looking for 2 or more years contracts that may require re-negotiations/price adjustments due to future changing economic variables

o   Regression analysis is best used for less competitive "Service Provider" or "customized solution" tenders where face-to-face negotiations are required.

Limitations of this Tool

Let's be clear. Regression analysis will help the negotiator see patterns and relationships in the data. This is a lever that needs to be skillfully utilised and deployed by a professional and prepared negotiator. Regression analysis will not by itself directly deliver savings. It will however help lift the 'fog of opportunity' giving more clarity for the negotiator. A well formulated regression is a good logical base for negotiations as it will identify the most important variables for negotiation, It still has the following limitations:

•   It is limited by the amount and quality of data/information available to run the model. The more the relevant data available, the better the model can predict. Remember Garbage In Garbage Out (GIGO). Ensure you strike a good balance between data accuracy, time and cost.

•   While Regression will give user (owner/contractor) a logical basis for negotiations, the actual result of the negotiations depends on the negotiator's level of preparation and skill to influence the user (Contractor/owner) to see the logic.

Cost Estimation for Maintenanace Outsourcing Model – An Alternative Approach

Estimation of costs for maintenance contracts is a complex process and is important for both the user/owners and the service providers for economic viability. Owners may pay a larger sum of money than actual maintenance costs. Alternatively, the service providers may be required to spend an excess amount of money because of the unreliable system performance. This situation occurs when the reliability of the asset or equipment and/or the maintenance cost parameters have not been modeled properly.

These models can be applied to outsourcing maintenance service for repairable systems. These models can be further extended by including provisions for used items, and utility functions for linking owner/agent's risk preferences and more complex models could be developed linking downtime.

This Section demonstrates the development of a conceptual cost model considering a simple maintenance contract policy in which, the contract terminates when contract period reaches a time or usage level L. The contract includes provision for corrective maintenance – rectification on failure as well as constant interval preventive maintenance actions to prolong the system reliability. This can be presented graphically by the Fig IV. Preventive maintenance actions are carried out at constant interval x, each PM restores the reliability of the asset to some extent. Between two successive preventive maintenances there could be one or more minimal corrective actions.

The following assumptions are made for model simplification purpose

- Failure rate increases with time/usage
- All corrective rectifications other than replacement are minimal repairs.
- Preventive maintenance actions are taken at constant interval (x)
- PM restores life to some extent.
- The level of restoration depends on the type and quality of the maintenance performed.

- Age restoration after each preventive maintenance (PM) is constant.

- All cost factors are constant over the contract period.

Total cost of contract over the contract period L can be expressed as-

$$C_T = C_m + C_i + C_r + p \qquad\qquad 1$$

Graphical representation of Maintenance Contract

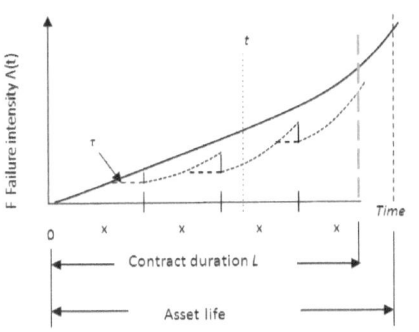

Where,
C_T: Total cost of maintenance contract
Cm: Cost of maintenance over the contract period
C_i: Inspection cost
C_r: Cost of risk associated with accident
p: Penalty Costs for not conforming to the contract and failure to meet agreed safety, reliability and availability standards.

Fig-IV

A. Estimating Maintenance Cost (C_m)

Expected total cost of maintenance service = (Expected total cost of all minimal corrective repairs over the contract + Expected cost of preventive maintenances over the contract L)/$(1+r)^n$

Where, r is the discount rate over the period n and n =1, 2, 3,

Expected cost of minimal repair: $C_{mr} = \sum_{k=0}^{n+1} \int_{kx}^{(k+1)x} \wedge(t-k\tau)dt$ \qquad 2

Expected cost of preventive maintenance during the contract NC$_{pm}$ \qquad 3

The total expected maintenance cost $C_m = \dfrac{\left[Cmr\sum_{k=0}^{n+1}\int_{kx}^{(k+1)x} \wedge(t-k\tau)dt + NCpm \right]}{(1+r)^n}$

Where, failure intensity $\wedge pm(t) = \wedge(t-k\,\tau)$

$\wedge pm(t)$: failure rate at time t, with maintenance.

$\wedge(t)$: original failure rate at time t when no maintenance is performed.

N: number of times maintenance is performed (including replacement).

x: fixed time interval of maintenance.

k: kth PM, k = 1,2,3,......... τ: restoration out of maintenance action.

τ = αx here, α is the quality of the maintenance

B. Estimating Inspection Cost (C_i)

Total inspection cost (C_i) over the contract can be given by

$$C_j = \{\sum_{j=0}^{N_i} c_i / (1+r_i)^j\} Xr / \{1 - (\frac{1}{(1+r)^n})\}$$

Where, N_i = Integer $[L/I_f]$

Ni is the expected number of inspection during the contract, and ri is the discounting rate associated with inspection interval. If is the inspection interval and r is the annual discount rate.

C. Estimating Risk Costs (Cr)

The risk cost associated with system failure and accident is based on the probability of inspection detecting potential failures and failures not being detected by inspection, accident and associated costs. This can be expressed as

$$C_R = \frac{\sum_{n=0}^{L} E[N(t_n, t_{n+1})] * [P_n(B) * b + (1 - P_n(B)) * (P_n(A) * a]}{(1+r)^n}$$

Where, a is the expected cost per accident;

b is the expected cost of repairing potential failure based on NDT

Pn(B) is the probability of detecting potential failure using NDT,

Pn(A) is the probability of undetected potential failure leading to accident during the interval between nth and (n+1)th periods

E[N(tn+1, tn)] is the expected number of failure over the interval of nth and n+1th year.

D. Total Cost of Maintenance Contract and the Service Providers Premium Charge (CT)

Therefore, the expected total cost of contract can be obtained by adding all the above costs. The service providers can charge a premium for such service by adding a profit with the total cost of servicing divided by the contract period (number of years/months or usage in thousands hours or Million gross tonnes). This can be expressed by Total cost of maintenance contract:

$$C_T = \frac{\left[Cmr(\sum_{k=0}^{N+1} \int_{kx}^{(k+1)x} \wedge \left(t - k\tau \right) dt) + CpmN_i \right]}{\left(1+r \right)^n} + \{ \sum_{j=1}^{N_i} c_i / \left(1+r_i \right)^j \} Xr / \{ 1 - (\frac{1}{\left(1+r \right)^n}) \} +$$

$$\frac{\sum_{n=0}^{N} E\left[N\left(t_n, t_{n+1} \right) \right] * [P_n(B)*b + \left(1 - P_n(B) \right) * (P_n(A)*a]}{\left(1+r \right)^n} + P$$

Service provider's premium charge per unit Year of contract can be expressed by:

$$Pc = C_T + P/L$$

where, L is the contract period of the Asset and P is the total profit marked up by the service provider. These equations can be solved by using Mathematical softwares such as MATLAB with all the available data.

Perquisite for Maintenance Outsourcing

The general findings of this study having implications for outsourcing Maintenance functions may be summarized as follows:

- Determining the extent to which a function should be outsourced is a complex undertaking and must involve the use of multidimensional factors and evaluation criteria, rather than reliance on direct costing alone.

- Partial outsourcing can be a viable alternative for entire spectrum ranging from 100% outsourcing to 100% in-house performance of functions. The tendency to polarize sourcing on an all or nothing at all basis inhibits effective outsource decision-making.

- The direct cost savings associated with outsourcing the maintenance studied have generally been small. Meager direct cost savings in the short run may also be expected in maintenance outsourcing functions. When indirect transaction costs are considered, significant cost savings are likely in noncore competency areas over time.

- Core competencies of an organization are typically few in number. It is arguable whether any of the functions under consideration represent a core competency of company. The tendency to view all functions as core competencies tends to inhibit effective outsource decision making.

- There is no evidence to suggest that there are necessary qualities or other differences between work performed in-house and outsourced work. Differences vary by function, vendors. and the effectiveness of contract management by the outsourcing organization.

- Evidence suggests that outsourcing organizations become more satisfied with outsourcing after a three to five year period. This trend may be due to organization re-engineering to effect outsourcing, or to more effective contract management over time.

- Functions do not tend to be brought back in-house once they have been outsourced. Outsourcing increased, rather than declined, over time relative to the functions studied.

- Effective contract management is a necessary ingredient in successful outsourcing. Likewise, effective partnering with suppliers can make the difference in outsourcing success.

- Traditional direct costing tends to be an ineffective indicator determining the extent to which a function should be outsourced. Outsource decision making is more effective when a constellation of relevant factors are considered.

- A true cost-benefit analysis of functions is difficult when deciding to outsource a function or perform it in-house. True cost-benefit analysis involves a consideration of transaction costs; that is all actual and potential, internal and external, direct and indirect, tangible and intangible, discretionary and nondiscretionary costs associated with an outsourcing/in-house transaction.

- Outsourcing can negatively impact an organization's in-house capability to deliver. In the event that the outsourced function is not a core competency of the organization, such impact may be problematic.

- Outsourcing is justified when the function in question is not a core competency of the organization and when the overall impact of outsourcing on the organization is positive.

- Pilot studies are valuable adjuncts to the outsourcing decision making process. Such studies may indicate the extent to which a function should be outsourced over time.

Even in light of the above described trends, Company often lacks sufficient information necessary to (a) fully evaluate the effectiveness of functions which have been outsourced, and (b) make effective decisions regarding future outsourcing. Through intensive overall discussion and review, seeking to answer such questions as:

- What functions have been outsourced & What cost savings have been accomplished by outsourcing these functions?

- What additional costs have been incurred due to outsourcing these functions?

- How have costs of outsourcing escalated after the initial contract period?

- What quality differences, if any, exist between in-house and outsourced work?

- Of the agencies or organizations that have outsourced, how satisfied are they after 3-5 years?

- What outsourced functions have been brought back in-house?

- What functions are most efficient to outsource and what functions should be done in-house?

- Is a cost benefit analysis of the outsource/in-house functions possible?

- What impact does outsourcing have on in-house capabilities?

- How do costs for outsourced functions vary as in-house capabilities are lost?

- When is outsourcing justified?

- What outsourcing legislation affects company efficiency?

The holistic approach is advised to be adopted while study, to determine and evaluate the long term impact and cost effectiveness of outsourcing certain functions.

It won't be out of place to put here what I strongly feel here is to know the best school for kid is not one with best infrastructure and attractive advt. with underpaid teacher working for extra hours with minimum or low facility. But school with good knowledgeable teachers with matching emoluments and moderate facilities.

Same can be story in maintenance outsourcing also. Services at sites are depending directly upon the people deputed at location. What is the knowledge level and technical skills of team deputed at site? How is there salary structure and facility in terms of leaves, medical, accommodation etc?

Rather than using one opinion to decide qualification and experience for any position, analytics to be employed to decide the right combination for the job. It has been observed that Industry usually fix up the qualification and experience of different position and defined in contract document with salary component, left on service provider.

Taking all aspects as above some time gives rise to unrealistic combination of salary, experience and qualification affecting performance as whole. Contractor to be asked for supplying cost of direct cost at site as execution. This shall comprise of Site Salary, Tools tackles and other infrastructure cost at site.

Ratio of direct cost at site to billing value can be considered (with appropriate profit provisioning) to understand back office cost leverage against it. It would give indication of how much excessive cost is pushed to back office contributing to plane cost (i.e. Cost of project managers, visits and commercials and other management cost).

In a study carried out among enterprises with applied outsourcing in their operations, author have carried out the finding on which outsourcing can improve a firm's cost-efficiency. Nevertheless the existing literature show that outsourcing improved their productivity and profitability. Previous researches has shown outsource activities to third party are proven to generate more productivity in businesses. The objectives of outsourcing are to cut cost, enhancing productivity and time saving. Outsourcing shall provide cost reduction to firm. This happen when the cost of upgrading maintenance in house is higher compare to outsourcing activities of hiring the third party expertise. For example, it has been found that factors affected by outsourcing decisions are sharing risk on technology investment, operating cost reduction, access to specialized expertise, fixed cost due to the contract, and perception of efficiency. In addition, examining the reason firm apply outsourcing is because it can increased capacity, higher quality of product and service and reduced cost. Other outsourcing motivations besides reasons of cost and quality is a political and historical reason based on experience elsewhere in the business specifically influence of parent companies.

Selection of Maintenance Contractors

The selection of maintenance contractors depends on their ability. The general criteria governing the selection of contractor include reputation; geographical position; perceived quality of services; contractor resources; workload and availability; technical excellence; and low price.

Contracts of Maintenance Services Maintenance contracts can be classified into three types. A description of each is provided as follows:

- Performance contracts: This applies where the complete maintenance services are awarded to a contractor. Some percentage of fees in these contracts is linked with performance parameters and released only on attaining KPI associated with those parameters.

- Facilitator contracts: The client is only the user of the physical assets, whereas they are owned and maintained by the contractors.

- Work-package contracts: Design and planning of the maintenance are performed by the client, who informs the contractors about the time that is needed to do maintenance services.

Moreover, maintenance can be organized by a variety of contracts. These contracts are as follows:

- Fixed price contracts: The price is agreed and fixed before the contract is signed.

- Lump sum contracts: The contractor receives a set amount as payment for delivering works to the owner. The contract price includes the contractor's reimbursement and his profit.

- Term contracts: The contractor must carry out certain types of work within certain limits of cost for an agreed period. The work is usually priced on either a measured term or day-work term.

- Cost plus contract: three types exist in this category. These include cost plus fixed contracts, where the contractor is reimbursed for actual allowable costs, and he receives a fixed percentage of the contract value as his fee or profit; cost plus fluctuating free contracts, where the contractor is paid the actual cost of the work plus a fee; and cost plus percentage contracts, where the contractor is paid the actual cost of the work, plus an agreed percentage of the actual cost.

In a general attempt to make all contract to single window, contract cell and SCM needs to pay attention is what is the services directly provided by service provider and other services subcontracted by main contractor. For service offloaded by contractor to some other agency the increase in chain leads to somewhat not only weaken the governance but also cause leakage of cost.

Industry leaders can't expect to have the upper hand in an outsourcing negotiation. Whether you're negotiating the initial contract, an extension or a change order, the outsourcer normally has the advantage.

That's because outsourcers are involved in just such negotiations all the time. They understand the internal cost structure and frequently negotiate for the same set of services using the same pricing mechanisms and contract. You might level the playing field a bit if your company is large enough to have a dedicated contract management cell, but you will still be at a disadvantage. Your vendor management group does indeed focus entirely on negotiating pricing, but it does it for everything from stationary, Hardware to complex outsourcing arrangements. Its focus is much more diffuse than that of the people on the other side of the table. And since pricing mechanisms, sales channels and service levels vary by outsourcer, it's difficult to master the nuances of every vendor's contract terms.

But one way to get the best outsourcing deal you can is to make it clear to the vendors that you understand how they make money. That sort of knowledge can position you to make intelligent decisions that can lower your costs by lowering the outsourcer's costs.

So what are some of the cost-reducing techniques that outsourcers use? They include the following:

Purchase aggregation. The large amount of products (Tools, PPE, consumable etc.)and services that outsourcers purchase in support of their clients allows them to obtain lower prices than all but the largest enterprises. Expert house, Consultants, trainings and other service contractors typically offer significant discounts on rate contract and volume sales. Outsourcers also benefit from aggregating supplies, shipping and other services. For example, companies that fix any equipment in a repair shop obtain excellent freight rates based on the large amount of equipment that moves from the customer to the repair facility and back.

In addition to products and services, outsourcers hire engineers, database analysts and other technical specialists, which they spread across multiple clients. While very large organizations can justify the cost of technical specialists, small and mid-tier organizations often struggle to match specialist capacity with demand.

Evaluate which products and services could benefit from volume pricing when deciding which tasks to outsource. Some organizations, particularly smaller ones, will find it beneficial to expand the outsourcing scope to take advantage of expensive but hard-to-find technical specialists. Technical specialized activities are catered by different OEM AMC with fixed and emergency visits.

Internal efficiency. Outsourcers streamline internal processes and technology platforms wherever possible. Implementing standardization reduces internal labor costs while making it easier to deliver consistent, high performance – ISO 55000 for Effective asset management, ISO 50000 – Energy Management systems, ISO 9000 quality service&. Internal operations are typically based on industry-standard practices such as, PMI's certifications or virtualization. All are well understood by maintenance professionals, easily explained to executive management and supported by numerous tools.

Embracing the outsourcer's practices and tools promotes efficiency in both the outsourcer and the client. If you are unwilling to adopt the outsourcer's practices, you are unlikely to get all of the hoped-for benefits from outsourcing. Discuss process standardization before signing the contract. If your processes need revamping, work with the outsourcer to decide if it will be cheaper for you or the outsourcer to do the work. There is no point in redesigning your processes twice.

Facility costs. Some outsourcers allocate insurance, taxes and other facility costs proportionally across current customers. This works well when the data center, service desk or repair center is operating at capacity but can result in higher costs when customers leave or contracts are completed.

Evaluate the cost of doing business in the area in which your services will be performed. Labor, power, land, and other costs vary widely. And be careful to limit pass-through cost increases during negotiations.

Technical resource leverage. Some industries may require a variety of specialized skills such as Engineers, database analysts and network analysts. Technical tools and authentic licenses required may include perimeter security, communications equipment and network discovery appliances. Very large organizations can justify the cost of both the staff and the tools. Small and mid-tier organizations, often struggle with both. Since most employees prefer full-time employment, demand for technical skills rarely matches the exact capacity of staff. As a result, technical specialists are frequently either overworked or searching for projects to avoid boredom. Similarly, even if specialized technical tools are available, they are often used infrequently or significantly below full capacity.

Outsourcers spread people and tools across multiple clients, better matching capacity to demand. In addition, since outsourcing is the business, technical staffers are offered more diverse career opportunities. Unless you are large enough to justify a deep technical bench, consider insourcing the design of your technical environment but outsourcing the day-to-day operation and maintenance of that environment.

Salary arbitrage. Many outsourcers staff positions not requiring face-to-face interaction in low-cost parts of the world. Typically, this works best with well-structured processes requiring interaction with other technical staff. It is minimally beneficial with less structured processes or when the outsourcer must communicate regularly with nontechnical staff. Before accepting support from a low-cost part of the world, make sure your processes are well structured and ascertain that no language, time zone or cultural differences will hinder performance.

Clearly, lowered cost is only one consideration in an outsourcing decision. But if you pursue outsourcing, you obviously want to negotiate the best price possible. Do not mindlessly beat your outsourcers to lower their prices! Allow them to assume responsibility for parts of your operation that enable them to leverage their scale, expertise and cost structure. Doing so can ultimately reduce costs for both of you, and your outsourcer will be grateful for being able to negotiate win-win pricing. Don't start your long-term relationship as adversaries; show from the beginning that you intend to be collaborative partners.

Cost Review During Contract Renewal, Change

This forms the most complex part of process, with two apparent parties (i.e. Contractor & Organization) with internal sub team (Technical and BA Business Administration). The function of each can be elaborated as below:

1. Organization – Technical: This is the direct customer for services and want in the form of best service, in shortest time, Minimum rework, Expert at the short notice, continuous improvement and modifications, with strong penalties against non-deliverables and long list of wishful thinking.

2. Organization–BA: This function is to support their technical counterpart at the lowest possible cost. With strong KPI associated with imposing penalty for any deviation from KPI.

3. Contractor – Technical: They are the service centre providing services directly and work on the demand of Organization technical within the business framework of signed contract.

4. Contractor-BA: This function forms guardians of management policy and responsible to impose the same appropriately and provide feedback to management towards business updates.

5. Others: In addition to above other functions of both contractor and organizations into communication may be sales & BD, stores, Safety and security etc. can be classified to either category based on hierarchy structure.

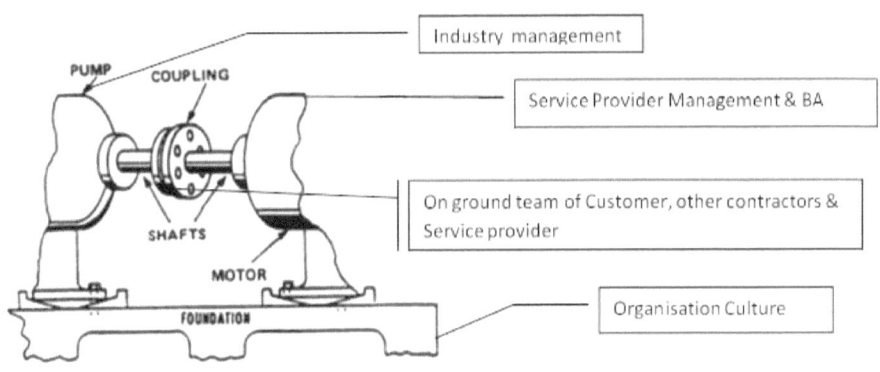

Fig – V

As it is evident from the above model Fig-V, if technical team at shop floor represented by coupling and Organization BA act as Load (Pump) and Contractor BA (Motor) as drive. Foundation here represent the Organization culture. The objective is same to transfer the value across the business efficiently with minimizing losses.

There are three possible situations for any contract as:

1. Contract is first time contract after completion of project: with no prior references or, and the experience of deployed team is input for drafting and execution of contract. Processing these contracts to establish contractor after good negotiation can be best strategy to stabilize the system and map the skill and competency of contractor.

2. Transferring the existing in house operation to outsource: These are most difficult to materialize as Customer here has clear idea of job and associated cost with issues and problems and price quoted by contractor always appears to be on higher side.

   It is recommended for customer to consider logistic, personal and local site issues, regional issues i.e. labor problems etc. on realistic parameter to take such decisions.

3. Contract renewal to same contractor or change contractor: Here is an opportunity of true assessment of performance in past and add on additional scope/activity with incorporating necessary

change. On one hand, it is required to true evaluation of existing contractor on different dimensions and rate on predefined scale and on other hand give fair opportunity to new vendor to prove on level ground.

In case of new contractor, please ensure for sharing all necessary information and discuss for any reason for price variance. Existing contractor are anyway on advantage for running contract.

Profit sharing model: In the current competitive scenario, this model can be better choice with increased corporation and trust with strong long lasting relationship. i.e. It can act both way as:

1. In case of there is any saving in term of Energy, spare or increased Production on account of improvement of reliability certain percentage of profit by owner can be shared with service provider for definite period.

2. On the same line if margins are increased beyond predefined range after keeping all future provisions intact some percent of excess can be shared by service provider with owner in terms of providing additional service with zero invoices.

Although it is an attempt of goodwill gesture they should not be a part of written contract but can be included in internal planning strategy with formulae devised for calculations.

VIEWPOINT

- Maintenance Cost can be bench marked, reviewing maintenance cost of previous years, or other contract cost for other services in the past.

- In case of new project without any past history benchmark to be framed referring to industrial standards (for specific industry) as% of capital cost/production, prevalent at that time.

Chapter 4

Contract Framing and Collaboration

It is impossible to unsign a contract, so do all your thinking before you Sign.

— **Warren Buffet**

Introduction

This is the most important constituent of any outsourcing business, which commences with framing tender and ends with the signing of contracts. In some of the cases, it has been observed that Industry going for outsourcing services has no clarity of scope and assumes entire maintenance within the premises to be contractor responsibility giving rise to a lot of ambiguity which later turns into conflicts. Effective contract management is a necessary ingredient in successful outsourcing. Likewise, effective partnering with a service provider can make outsourcing experience, altogether different.

Indian Contract Act 1872

Objective of the act: The objective of the contract act is to ensure that right and obligations arising out of a contract are honored and the legal remedies are made available to an aggrieved party against the party failing to honour his part of agreement. The Indian contract act makes it obligatory that this is done and compels the defaulter to honour their commitments.

Steps Involved in Contract

- Proposal and its communication
- Acceptance of proposal and its communication
- Agreement by mutual promises
- Contract
- Performance of contract

Essential elements of a valid contract:

- Proper Offer and its acceptance
- Free consent of both parties
- Mutual and lawful consideration for agreement
- It should be enforceable by law. Hence, intention should be to create legal relationship. Agreements of social and domestic nature are not contracts
- Parties should be competent to contract
- Object should be lawful
- Certainty and possibility of performance.
- Contract should not be declared as void under contract act or any other law.

Distinction between agreement and contract

Agreement	Contract
Offer and its acceptance constitute an agreement.	Agreement and its enforceability constitute a contract.
An agreement may or may not create a legal obligation.	A contract necessarily creates a legal obligation.
Every agreement need not necessarily be a contract.	All contracts are necessarily agreements.
Agreement is not concluded or binding contract.	Contract is concluded and binding on the concerned parties.

These are moreover expressed contract.

Maintenance Service Contract A MSC is a legal document that is binding on both parties and it needs to deal with technical, economic, and legal issues. Classification of contracts

1. Standard contracts: Mainly in the form of extended warranties for consumer products and service contracts for commercial and industrial products (e.g., lifts in buildings and other plant equipment). The service provider taking into account the marketing aspects determines the terms of the contract. These are vendor-centered contracts and initially drafted by the Supplier/Service provider.

2. Customized contracts: For complex plants and infrastructures where the owner and the terms often initiate the contract decided jointly. These are customer-centered contracts, initiated as inquiry/ RFQ by owner.

Technical Issues

- Types of maintenance tasks (PM and/or CM) to be carried out and any additional service requirement.
- The details of the tasks to be carried out. With exclusions properly enlisted
- Types of the component/piece parts used for maintenance (standard part, Part manufacturing approved part, etc.)
- Mobilization
- Turnaround time
- Documentations
- KPI

Economic/Financial Issues

- Payments
- Penalties
- Risks
- Insurance

Legal Issues

- Terms of contract
- Contract duration
- Dispute resolution
- Guaranty/warranty
- Force major issues

Unless the contract is written properly with all relevant data (relating to the object and collected by the service agent) are analyzed properly by the customer, the long-term costs and risks will escalate.

Although maintenance contracts are complex and the possibility of any unanticipated condition cannot be ruled out. Successful Maintenance contracts are an outcome of good faith and established trust between customer and service provider attaining win-win conditions for both.

Whenever a contract is drawn between any customer and vendor, regardless of the industry, the Scope of Work (or Statement of Work) agreement forms guidelines clearly defining expectation out of the contract. The Scope of Work (SOW) is a formal document that describes the work activities, deliverables, timelines and milestones, pricing, quality requirements, and governance terms and conditions, etc. Whether you are a project manager, a marketing professional, or a government executive, you would be necessarily dealing with the external world for project contracts, vendor selection, sales and support, customer service, and many other activities. The SOW gives both the vendor and the customer, a clear picture of the complete project requirements so that both parties are on the same ground.

To develop a Scope of Requirements (SOR) for the Goods and or Services required ensuring a full and detailed tender is produced with appropriate scoring. It is important to remember that SoR's are used to support the tender which is assessing the capability, capacity, and commerciality of the bidders.

The SOR doesn't need to provide too much detail as this could potentially create issues in terms of determining the winning bidder. It is often easier to imagine your tender as the 'exam' paper to assess the bidders' capability, capacity, and commerciality against your SOR.

Try to write your SOR in a sufficiently detailed manner, to provide enough of a basis at a later stage when you will be required to extract relevant criteria that will be used to differentiate competing proposals. Remember that the selection criteria that you develop for your tender must have a logical foundation. For example, you cannot differentiate bidders on factors that would exclude others such as based on specific brands and or services that would unfairly exclude others.

If writing a performance-based SOR, try not to "tie the Bidders' hands" by being overly prescriptive in your description of the work and the manner in which it is to be undertaken. While care should always be taken to fully describe your requirement, try to balance this by leaving bidders with the flexibility in their proposals to offer innovative and environmental considerations and strategies and to accept maximum responsibility and accountability for the results of their work.

While writing SOR, one needs to think ahead to the contract award and management stage (once the winning bidder has been selected and the work is underway). In doing this, try to write your SOR in such a way as to ensure that the mutual expectations of the resulting contract will be adequately described and easily understood. Once the contract is underway, a well written SOR will go a long way to minimizing potential misunderstandings and/or disputes with your service provider.

Remember to always use generic (non-proprietary) terminology and references in describing your requirements. This enables greater competition, and it also minimizes the risk of a bid challenge or allegation that the requirements were slanted to a particular bidder.

There is tremendous potential within a SOR for overlap, duplication, and/or contradiction with the Terms and Conditions (T&C's) of the resulting contract. Remember – the contents of the SOR are variable to define the requirements at hand vs the t&c's which contain the standard terms and conditions of the resulting contract. If it's covered-off in the t&c's, you generally don't need to worry about it in the SOR.

Above all, do your best in the SOR to convey to the Bidders what it will take on their part to execute the work to your satisfaction, and accordingly what it will take for them to ultimately have their work accepted and certified for payment.

The five-point guideline, as outlined in maintenance Outsourcing: Five Rules That Will Transform Outsourcing are:

a. Focus on outcomes. The idea is to move away from buying and selling transactions to a new level of cooperation.

b. Focus on the **WHAT**, not the **HOW**. Companies can often fall into the trap of tightly defined statements of work (SOWs) that strictly define HOW, rather than focus on objectives they want to accomplish.

c. Jointly formulate clearly defined and measurable results based on collaboration and alignment.

d. Jointly negotiate pricing models that include incentives based on performance rather than making an additional service sale or hiring lowest-cost labor.

e. The partnership should have a governance framework that provides insight into the nature of the relationship and its objectives so that transition, management protocols, and incentives implement continuous improvement and achieve desired results.

Let's understand the above concept and the guidelines in more detail. As the defined approach to fit appropriately with companies that want to develop effective, long-term performance partnerships where both parties have a stake in maintaining the relationship.

While no two relationships are alike, the most effective ones achieve a partnership based on optimizing for innovation and improved service, reduced cost to the company outsourcing, and improved profits to the service provider. The trend toward performance partnerships has evolved— companies and service providers work together to develop performance-based solutions where their interests are aligned. Both parties receive tangible benefits, either through tangible or intangible incentives.

Agreement on desired outcomes forms the basis of the contract. Under this framework, the service provider is challenged to apply "Technology know-how" and/or investments to the relationship. It also takes on risk to do it, in essence putting "skin in the game." The service provider looks at how it can best apply world-class processes, technologies, and capabilities that will drive value to the company that is outsourcing.

i.   Adopt an outcome-based versus transaction-based business model traditionally, many outsource arrangements are built around a transactional model. Most often this transaction-based model is coupled with a cost-plus or a competitively bid fixed price per transaction pricing model to ensure that the buyer is getting the lowest cost per transaction. Under this method, the service provider is paid for every transaction—regardless of whether or not it is needed. Thus, the more inefficient the entire process, the more money the service provider can make.

Conventional business models achieve the lowest cost for transactions for the company outsourcing. However, it often does not help the company accomplish what it really wants or needs. That's because the company that has outsourced gets what it contracted for, but what it really needed might fall short of an efficient and low-cost total-support solution.

The Vested model operates under an outcome-based model in which the provider aligns its interests to what the company really wants: an efficient, low-cost total solution. Aligning interests is a major element of the program. Instead of paying a provider for unit transactions for the various services provided—Such as technical and maintenance support hours, etc.—the company and its service provider agree upon desired performance outcomes. In essence, this model buys outcomes, not individual transactions.

ii.   Focus on the WHAT, not the HOW Adopting an Outsourcing business model does not change the nature of the work to be performed. What does change is the way in which the company purchases outsourced services? The buyer specifies its needs; the provider is responsible for determining "how" it all gets done. The most effective partnerships include minimal discussion of the processes that service providers must follow to meet the requirements. Instead, they focus on performance expectations. It's up to the service provider to figure out how to put the supporting pieces together to achieve the company's goals. Performance partnerships let each partner do what it does best.

iii.   Clearly define and measure the desired outcomes. The parties should clearly define and measure their desired outcomes. These outcomes are usually expressed in terms of a limited set of high-level metrics. Once the desired outcomes are agreed upon, the service provider can propose a solution that will deliver the required level of performance at a pre-determined price. Under this model, the outsourcing company pays only for results, i.e., Overall reliability, Energy saving, not transactions such as Servicing equipment, Replacing components. In turn, the service provider is paid for the value that its overall solution delivers, not for the activity performed. Carefully defining and measuring desired outcomes will position the relationship for success by ensuring the partners' mutual objectives are, in fact, being correctly addressed.

iv.   Optimize pricing model incentives for cost/service tradeoffs Proper structuring of the pricing model will incentivize an optimal cost/ service. A well-structured pricing model is based on the type of contract (i.e., fixed price or cost reimbursement) that will be used to reward the outsource service provider. In the establishment of a pricing model, businesses should apply two principles:

First, the model must balance risk and reward for both parties. The agreement is structured to ensure that the service provider assumes risk only for decisions within its control.

Second, a properly structured model will incentivize the service provider to solve customer problems proactively. The better the service provider is at solving the problems, the more incentives or profits it will make. Thus, providers are encouraged to develop innovative and cost-effective methods of performing work. The owner may insist on the provision to penalize for any shortcoming in KPI, for reason attributed to service provider performance. The model doesn't guarantee higher profits: It gives service providers the authority and autonomy to make investments in their process (es) and product reliability that can generate greater ROI than a more conventional cost-plus or fixed-price-per-transaction approach would provide.

v. The governance structure must emphasize insight versus oversight. In the early days of outsourcing, many organizations made the mistake of just throwing work over the fence to their service providers without fully defining the requirements or developing performance metrics or SLAs (service-level agreements). An effective partnership outsources processes to suppliers and service providers that are the real experts in those processes. These types of partnerships should be managed to create cultures of insight versus oversight.

Unfortunately, too many companies spend too much time and resources micromanaging their service providers. A sound governance structure will establish insight—not simply provide more layers of supervision.

A commitment to delivering against projected value for the company outsourcing—such as a commitment to reduce costs or improve service or both—shifts risk to the service provider. In exchange, the company that's outsourcing commits to allow the outsource provider to earn additional profit for achieving this incremental value. The result is a win-win vested partnership: a true trading-partner paradigm shift.

Scope of Requirements (SoR) - Sample

The following example SOR is designed to help 'subject matter experts' to work through their scope of requirements when looking at maintenance outsourcing. Once you've worked through the SOR you will need to arrange a meeting with Procurement who will advise and support the most appropriate method of service provider selection as required by the company procurement procedure.

1. TITLE

The Title clearly and succinctly summarizes the name of the requirement being contracted for, and should, 'at a glance', answer the question: who is trying to buy what and via what form of contracting. Briefly and clearly, identify the type of service being acquired, the organization (Department, Faculty, Office, etc.,) acquiring the services.

2. BACKGROUND

The Background section provides contextual information that plays a key role during the proposal solicitation stage by providing Bidders with an understanding of the organization's requirements, its objectives, and key drivers for the work to be undertaken that can assist in determining whether to bid and in preparing a Proposal. The Background section should also support the organization's documentation of its business case, including the rationale for the work and the need to enter into the contract.

    a. Describe the mandate of the organization (Department, Faculty, Office, etc.,) acquiring the services.

    b. As required, identify the authorized users of the resulting service/product. Describe the area within the organization (Faculty, Division, etc.,) requiring the services. Similarly, identify whether the resulting service/product will be accessible by all areas within the organization, or by only selected (and identified) authorized users.

    c. Describe the specific commodity (the type of service) being acquired.

d. At a strategic level, briefly describe the organizational program, project, or internal operational requirement for which the services are being acquired. The 'need' for the work to be completed must be clearly articulated – if possible, contextualize the project/requirement within the organization/area's overall business plan.

e. If available, and if it would be helpful to Bidders in developing their proposals to provide publicly accessible informational links such as website URL.

f. Identify whether the requirement is recurring, the first in a series of similar upcoming requirements, a subsequent phase in an upcoming project. This can add on providing commissioning support in upcoming project extension, execute preservation activity for commissioned plant delayed in operation or support for any other anticipated future work for which contracts will be established by the Owner at a later date, this should be clearly articulated, including any restrictions that may be placed on the resulting Service provider(s) from participating on the future work.

This subsection can help to mitigate the risk of perceived bias and/or prior knowledge on the part of the 'incumbent' Service provider, through the organization's proactive disclosure of its previous activities and future intentions. This will guide the prospective service provider to avoid any excessive contingency built up in cost.

3. OBJECTIVE

The Objective section identifies the organization's overall outcome for the resulting contracted work, to provide a clear understanding and enforceable outcome for the work to be undertaken. The Objective also identifies the organization's anticipated outcome of the competitive bidding process, leading to the awarding of the resulting contract(s). Its primary role at the tender stage is to provide Bidders with a clear understanding of the structure and number of resulting service/product(s) to be awarded.

a. Describe in outcomes-based terminology precisely what the organization hopes to achieve as a result of this tender.

b. Indicate if it is the organization's intent to award the resulting service/product(s) to one or multiple Suppliers.

c. Identify whether the required type of Service provider consists of a firm or an individual providing services, or both. What is preparedness for any unforeseen external support within short notice?

4. DEFINITIONS AND APPLICABLE DOCUMENTS

Definitions and Applicable Documents section provide contextual information at both the tender and contract stages to ensure clarity in the interpretation of the SOR and identification of overarching legislation, policies, procedures, and guidelines that will govern the resulting work. The purpose of this section is to mitigate ambiguity and misunderstanding that could lead to poor proposals at the tender stage, or default, breach or dispute at the contract stage.

5. BUSINESS AND/OR TECHNICAL ENVIRONMENT

Business and/or Technical Environment section provides contextual information to Bidders at the tender stage to identify operational requirements of the work and programs, systems, and infrastructure with which the Supplier(s) will be required to work in the contract stage.

6. DESCRIPTION AND SCOPE OF WORK

The Scope provides guidance at the tender stage to assist Bidders in understanding the work to be undertaken and provide clarity in developing their Proposals. At the contract stage, the Scope provides enforceable guidance to the Supplier as to where to focus its efforts in the resulting contract to ensure the Service provider remains 'in scope' and focused on issues, tasks, and other activities that are relevant to the completion of the work. The Scope section with a SOR describes the logical boundaries within which the work will take place (i.e. what is the work, and what is it not?). In contrast to the deliverables under the contract, which identify the specific, tangible items the Service provider must complete in order to receive payment, this section "sets the stage" for a later and more precise description of the deliverables, by first describing the work at a macro or conceptual framework level, and in more general terms.

Where deliverables may be characterized as Outputs of the resulting contract, the Scope identifies the Inputs (requirements of the broader field of work, specific activities, etc.) required to successfully complete the work.

Frame the required work within the context of the professional discipline in which it is situated. Provide a brief description of the discipline to ensure understanding of the requirements to successfully undertake the work within this broader field.

Clearly describe the activities the Service provider is required to undertake that will lead to the production of the deliverables, but that are not part of the content of the deliverables themselves. To ensure the contract remains "Performance-Based" do not over-specify the specific methodologies or approaches to be used in completing these required steps. Any organizational/requirement specific methodologies should be described appropriately.

For each activity described, provide the scale and metrics (e.g. identify the frequency, quantity or volume of inputs the Supplier is required to make) for the successful completion of the work. For anticipatory service all Scope activities will be "as required".

For Professional Services/Project Scopes of Work, identify the matching milestones. To avoid ambiguity or contradiction, direct Bidders/Suppliers for identification of where the deliverables fit within these phases/ milestones. For Scopes of Work where deliverables are unknown, the Scope may be driven by the type of Resource Categories required. In this instance, describe the typical activities associated with each of the Resource Category types.

7. DELIVERABLES

The deliverables section clearly identifies the tangible products or outcomes that the Supplier is required to produce in order to receive payment (i.e.

"Outputs"). In accordance with contracting policy, payment should be made only for the satisfactory completion of a concrete Deliverable or delivery of a service.

a. Clearly identify when payment will occur for the deliverables (i.e. at the end of the contract; upon receipt of the Deliverable; upon completion of the milestone; monthly; or otherwise). Payment is always conditional upon the satisfactory acceptance of the Deliverable(s). Clearly state this condition here.

b. Direct the Bidders/Supplier(s) to the subsequent sections of the SOR that will govern how the work is to be completed. This enhances the enforceability of the resulting mechanism at the contract stage by clearly linking the completion of the deliverables to the required resource quality, approach, performance standards, communications requirements, etc. The subsequent sections are critical at the contract stage and form an obligation on the Supplier in the successful completion of the work.

c. Payment could be split into two parts as fixed for infrastructure and variable on account of deliverables achieved.

8. SERVICE PROVIDER RESOURCE REQUIREMENTS AND QUALIFICATIONS (If required)

Service provider Resource Requirements and Qualifications section identify, in part, how the Service provider is required to undertake the work, by identifying the type of people (skill sets) the Service Provider is required to deploy and accountabilities for activities associated with each of the Service provides resources for the completion of the work. At the tender stage, this section provides guidance to the Bidders in relation to the organization's requirements and expectations; and it will also establish a foundation for developing selection and evaluation criteria within the tender. At the contract stage, it will be used to assess the suitability of the Supplier's deployed resources, providing the organization with a measure of enforceability for qualifications, in addition to providing enforceability for availability and replacement of named resources.

a. Clearly identify the Resource Categories required (e.g. Supervisor, Business Analyst, etc...) and their level of seniority in relation to the other Categories required.

b. Each Resource Category should be described in two (2) parts:

- description of the Resource Category's role and activities in the resulting work – This should NOT be written as a traditional "job description" (to avoid any appearance of an Employer-Employee relationship); and

- a description of the minimum required qualifications for an individual within the Resource Category to successfully undertake the work – Try to highlight the actual qualifications, skills, experience, and knowledge genuinely required by the Supplier's key resources needed to successfully and competently undertake the work, as described within the SOR.

Note: In some cases, qualifications, experience, and/or skill sets may not be specific to any one Resource Category. As needed, identify any specific skills/experience the Service provider, in general, is required to possess in order to complete the work. This information will also inform the development of the selection and evaluation criteria.

Clearly identify whether the resulting contract will allow for the completion of work by named resources only (i.e. only those individuals proposed and screened can complete the work) or whether any resource may be provided by the contractor provided that he/she meets the established requirements. If the former, in the event these resources are unavailable, the Service provider will be ineligible to receive the contract.

9. APPROACH AND METHODOLOGY

The Approach and Methodology describe how the Service provider will specifically go about the completion of the work under the resulting contract. Typically, in performance-based SoR's, and to mitigate the risk of liability for the organization in the event of a dispute or poor performance under the contract, the Service provider is required to provide its own specific methodology for the completion of the tasks and deliverables.

Bidders submit a proposed Approach and Methodology as part of their Proposal, which may be evaluated in the selection and evaluation criteria, and which, upon acceptance of the Proposal by the organization, becomes enforceable in the resulting contract.

Dependent upon the requirement, there may be portions of the Approach and Methodology that need to be prescribed to ensure conformity of the Contractor's work with existing government, industry, or discipline standards; or existing methodologies used within the organization. Where this is the case, take care to ensure that only those portions of the method that are essential are prescribed and that the Service provider retains creativity for innovation, and thus liability, for the implementation of its methodology and the resulting outputs.

However, in case of performance not meeting the requirement, the owner may initially give warning to the contractor to improve on it and thereafter have the liberty to execute the job from any external vendor to his satisfaction level and service charge of an external vendor to be debited from the contractor.

10. PERFORMANCE STANDARDS AND QUALITY ASSURANCE

Within any contract, there is an inherent performance standard that failure on the part of the Supplier to complete the required deliverables will result in the withholding of payment and/or determination of a breach of contract and/or default on the part of the Supplier.

Clearly identify this expectation and the associated role of the contract Operator/Manager who is responsible for determining the compliance of Supplier deliverables with the Performance Standard of responsiveness, timely completion, and quality work. In the event of a dispute, this section must be clear enough to enable the withholding of payment under the contract for poor performance.

Consider: −

- Speed/timeliness of service delivery or work completion;
- Technical conformity of the product/service/work to specification (i.e. functionality, accuracy, and completeness);

- Accessibility of the Supplier (e.g. for Client Services contracts);

- Client satisfaction with the Supplier's level of service (as assessed by a client satisfaction index).

11. REPORTING AND COMMUNICATIONS

Reporting and Communications section describes the obligations of the Service provider to maintain contact with the organization during the resulting contract. It also identifies any specific reports or other updates the Service provider will be required to provide during the course of the work, that is necessary to ensure product/service oversight and control.

12. RISKS AND CONSTRAINTS

This section identifies potential risks (real or perceived) that could incur in undertaking the work and any operational constraints that could impact the ability of the Service provider to complete the work and/or require consideration in the Service provider methodology. At the contract stage, identification of any Risks and Constraints in the SOR provides a degree of legal protection for the organization. Should any Risk that has been identified befall the Service Provider, or should a Constraint impede the Service provider ability to complete the work; previous transparency and disclosure of these items in the SOR can mitigate the organization's liability, as the Service provider has been informed of their potential and has accepted this in its offer to enter into and acceptance of the contract.

Clearly define the terms Risk and Constraints. A Risk is an unusual or exceptional peril (e.g. legal, physical, financial) that could befall the Service provider in the course of undertaking the work. A Constraint is an operational reality within the organization's environment that may impede the Service Provider's ability to complete its work.

Describe the specific Risk(s) (e.g. risk of physical harm, risk of third party litigation, etc.) that has the potential to occur. Clearly identify the responsibility of the Service provider to take appropriate measures to mitigate the aforementioned risk.

Describe the specific Constraint(s) (e.g. restricted access, time constraints, etc.) that is known or likely to impede the Service Provider's work. Clearly identify the responsibility of the Service Provider's to take appropriate measures to work within the Constraint(s). If the Work under the resulting product/service consists of planning and scoping for a future contractual requirement, it may be necessary to restrict the Bidder's ability to participate in any future related work.

13. SUPPLIER RESPONSIBILITIES

Beyond the Supplier's responsibility to complete the work under the contract in accordance with any defined methodology, performance standards, and constraints, there may be other specific items the Supplier is responsible to provide/ensure while completing the work. Supplier Responsibilities are itemized to help mitigate the risk to the organization of an employer-employee relationship arising under the contract.

14. LOCATION OF WORK AND TRAVEL

The location of work and travel specifies the geographic location(s) where the organization requires the delivery of services and whether/how any requirements for Supplier travel will be reimbursed by the organization under the resulting contract.

Define where the Supplier's work will take place (i.e. at either facility identified by the organization or at facilities of the Supplier's choosing, or both). If work will take place at organizational facilities, describe their location.

Clearly identify any requirement for the supplier to travel to locations other than the organization's place of business. If possible, specify anticipated locations, frequency, duration, number of resources, and schedule. Clearly describe any requirements for travel to locations that may be considered a Remote or 'Hardship' posting and any risks associated with such travel. If specific details are not yet known, provide enough information to identify the requirement. Identify whether no travel is anticipated under the resulting contract.

Identify whether the Supplier will be reimbursed for travel and/or living expenses to/from locations other than the organization's usual place of business. If travel is required, identify the Supplier's obligation to comply with the Travel policy with respect to the reimbursement of expenses.

Identify whether funding for travel will be added to the contract upon award or whether the Supplier's Proposal will form an estimate for travel costs. (If the latter, amounts for travel can form part of the evaluation process).

The maintenance service provider shall establish codes for uniform, vehicles including service vehicles as administrative protocols in consensus with the engaging agency and would have it approved by the engaging agency. A compliance report to these standard operating protocols is suggested to be submitted to the engaging agency on a periodic basis.

15. SECURITY REQUIREMENTS

This section of the SOR identifies requirements for the Supplier to comply with the organization's requirements under the Security policy. A Security Requirements Checklist may also be required and it is suggested to contact Service agencies to determine what is needed.

16. INTELLECTUAL PROPERTY/COPYRIGHT

This section of the SOR indicates which party will own or have rights to the existing intellectual property used to complete the work, and which party will own or have rights to any new intellectual property created as a result of the work (referred to as "foreground").

As a variety of pre-defined and often highly technical clauses are used in this section, employees should always seek input from Procurement (who will review with Legal if appropriate) prior to finalizing this section.

17. SUSTAINABLE PROCUREMENT AND SERVICES

This section of the SOR identifies requirements for the Service provider to comply with the organization's requirements under the Guideline on Socially Responsible Procurement.

or Identify any specific equality and environmental requirements (e.g. use of recycled materials, etc.) for the execution of the work.

The owner should provide guidelines for disposing of the waste and store the replaced spares with designated space on the premises.

18. COMMENCEMENT, DURATION, AND AWARD

This section of the SOR identifies the legal time frame for the resulting contract product/service and the commencement of work under the agreement. Identify the time period of the resulting product/service, from the date of legal award to the specific end date or within a specified duration.

Identify any rights reserved by the organization to extend the period of the resulting product/service, and for what duration.

19. INSURANCE/WARRANTIES

This section of the SOR identifies any legal obligations imposed on the Service provider in the resulting product/service in relation to the need to indemnify the organization (i.e. insurance), or the need to offer a warranty or guarantee. It is suggested to contact Legal Services to discuss any special requirements.

As required, describe the type of insurance required, and whether the Supplier is expected to indemnify the organization, and to what extent.

As required, describe any limitation on Supplier liability under the resulting contract.

As required, identify any specific liabilities the Supplier will be required to accept in completing the work under the contract.

As required, for goods and/or maintenance services, etc. identify any specific warranty or guarantee requirements, what is covered under the warranty/guarantee, to what standard, and for what time period.

However good contract shall precisely elaborate every aspect of scope, but in maintenance contract, the good faith between two parties play well. It should make associate/partnership synergy work between service providers instead of the master-slave relationship.

20. ADDITIONAL CLAUSES IN A CONTRACT

These are Some of the condition may be included in the tender document but service provider shall definitely insist to include in their offer and final signed agreement.

Arbitration: This section defines the guidelines for any dispute resolution, which initially is with mutual consent in the party aligned with the law of land. i.e. for such arbitration proceedings will be held in consonance with the provisions of arbitration and conciliation act of 1996 or any statutory modification or re-enactment thereof for the time being in force.

Limitation of liability: This clause limits the liability of Service providers to a certain percentage of fees to avoid exposure to unlimited liability.

Force Majeure: This clause elaborates on the action in the time of crisis and includes all possible adversities causing an interruption in service. Can be worded as-

"In the event of, stoppage of work in any establishment of ours/our vendors during the execution period owing to war hostilities, acts of the public enmity, civil commotion, riots, acts of terrorism, sabotage, fires, floods, power cuts, earthquake, tempests, explosions, epidemics or any acts of God, quarantine restrictions, strikes, lockouts, trade disputes, the concerted action of workmen, breakdowns, accidents, etc. as well as transport embargoes, failures or delays in transportation, Governmental decree and/or causes beyond our control, deliveries/services may be postponed partially or wholly canceled by Service provider."

The Service Provider (Collaborating the Growth)

The partnership is a tailored business relationship based on mutual trust, openness, shared risk, and the firms individually would achieve shared rewards that yield a competitive advantage, resulting in business performance greater than would be achieved by firm individually. Partnering may be among competitors or non-competitors and may exist for strategic or operational reasons. Although all partners share basic attributes of a mix of features and of markets, they come in a myriad of different structural forms. These different structures affect the pattern of decision-making and the control of capabilities.

A customer – service provider relationship is also important in maintaining the strategic leadership of an organization. The customer – service provider partnership relationship will be advantageous to both customer and service provider without sacrificing each other's independence and identity. It will be a "win-win" situation where both will grow together by helping each other, sharing risk, information, technology, knowledge and capital to maintain growth and profitability. These relationships generally exist in order to improve operating procedures and efficiency; thus they are classified as cooperative arrangements to the extent relationships exist to ensure efficient operation of an asset throughout its complete lifecycle, the relationship may go beyond cooperation to include collaboration.

Following factors can be considered as elements for a successful partnership:

- communications,
- early warning,
- joint operating controls,
- risk/reward sharing,
- trust and commitment to each other's success,
- contract style (time frame and coverage),
- scope (share partner's business, value-added, and critical activities), and
- investment (financial, technology, and people).

The partnership is an arrangement for mutual benefits and is based on trust and cooperation. Therefore, it is important to make sure that both parties are benefitted from the alliance. It has been evident that the most important factor contributing to the failure of a partnership alliance is poor communication between the partners. Other factors contributing to failure are a lack of trust, poor up-front planning, and a lack of shared goals.

Developing and Implementing Partnership

a. Identification of a need for partnering: Top management, based on the competitive strategic plan of the firm, identifies the need for such partnership. Also, the need could be identified based on the environmental analysis or could come filtered through any functional area Establishing the strategic need and top management support is crucial to the success of the partnership.

b. Formation of a team of representatives from major functional areas: A team should be formed with representation from all major functional areas that will be affected by the choice of a service provider.

c. Additional needs analysis: The team should analyze and substantiate the need for partnering as opposed to other contractual relationships or an arm's length relationship. In addition, the team should submit the findings to the top management for additional support.

d. Determination of selection criteria: The team should determine the criteria of importance to the firm. It should include all such traditional service provider selection criteria as quality, availability, capability, cost, etc. In addition to those, other qualities such as cultural compatibility and top management compatibility should also be considered. An important aspect in this step is that the list must be developed and debated and approved before the selection process is started.

e. Development of the list of potential suppliers: After the criteria are established, a list of potential service providers who can meet the criteria should be developed. This list may include service agencies with whom the organization has had previous business deals. This list also should come from all departments who have some knowledge of suppliers' capability and had some experience with them.

f. Screen Potential Partners: The next step is screening potential partners based on the developed criteria. The team should draw relative experience from all functional areas to evaluate potential partners. The team should rate the partners on a comparable scale across the potential list of suppliers. The supplier to be chosen for a purchasing partnership should be the one who meets or appears to have the ability to meet, all the perceived needs of the firm at an acceptable level.

g. Establish the Relationship: The goal is to establish the foundation on which an ongoing relationship is based; one that is based on mutual trust, sharing, and commitment. A partnership will work only if the relationship is mutually beneficial. In establishing a relationship, it is necessary to have a high level of interaction, and this is critical to the success of the partnership.

h. Evaluate the Relationship: The future viability of partnering relationships will likely become obvious from six to twelve months into the relationship. Partnership evaluation is an ongoing process and should be performed by a team. Based on the evaluation, several courses of action should be pursued. Actions such as continuous monitoring of the relationship and performance, further building or expanding the relationship, dissolving or reducing the scope of the relationship, or dissolving the partnership, because of unsatisfactory performance.

i. Choosing the Right Partner: Once the decision is made to form a partnership, the critical question becomes with whom to partner. Strategic partnerships should be a win-win relationship where both parties benefit from the alliance. The partnership should add value to the larger organization, as well as be beneficial to the smaller organization. Finding the perfect fit is not easy and takes time, but is absolutely critical if success is to be achieved. Therefore, the partner selection process is a diligent and time-consuming one. Seven key steps to ensure successful partnerships include:

- clearly identify the goals and objectives of the partnership,

- create a measurement process for each partner,

- commit the necessary resources,

- empower the leaders to get the job done,

- marshal internal resources and focus people on the alliance, and

By following the above steps, the likelihood of successful partnerships greatly increases. Partnership goals need to be identified beforehand, and the appropriate leaders must be chosen for the job.

The RFP should ask the "right questions" instead of simply the most questions. It should be structured for ease of review, but be unstructured enough for the firm's values and culture to become apparent.

It is suggested that the firm seeking a partner "do their homework". In other words, they should research potential partners in order to find out as much as possible beforehand. Seek out referrals from others that have worked with the firm. Finally, a site visit should be made to potential partners. A checklist should be brought to the visit to look over the company. The list should include such items as the professionalism of personnel and environment, competency of management, and security & safety consciousness of the facility.

The specific characteristics of the right partner are that the partner's needs, skills, and resources be completely complementary to those of the outsourcing firm. The partner should also be financially stable and well managed. Finally, the partner should have previous experience with partnerships. As experienced partners, they have moved up the learning curve at the expense of another partner.

There are three elements that are common to all successful partnerships: impact, intimacy, and vision. The impact is a partner's capability to deliver tangible results. Successful partnerships increase productivity, add value, and improve profitability. Intimacy relates to the level of closeness between the partners. Partners that are successful have a close ongoing relationship built on trust. Finally, successful partnerships have a common vision. The vision is a specific picture of what the partnership can achieve, and how it is going to get there.

Factors to consider in choosing a partner include when to partner, what companies should be considered as potential partners, what are the characteristics of a good partner, and what steps should be taken when making a decision. The key is to thoroughly investigate potential partners.

Negotiating the Contract

The negotiation process begins once a partner is selected. The interests of the two parties are typically both complementary and conflicting; therefore, it is necessary to have an effective negotiation process to address the common interests, and resolve any differences. For example, they both want to succeed and become a marketable product or process. Each recognizes its own strength and weakness and the benefits of the strategic alliance. On the other hand, there are clearly interests that differ. The Manufacturing unit interest lies in getting trouble-free operation of the plant at minimal cost with no botheration on associated issues of EHS, Manpower, etc. on the other hand service provider's main interest lies in resource optimization to attain customer deliverable at minimum cost. All necessary issues must be discussed and resolved in the negotiation phase in order for the alliance to be successful.

There are some important issues to keep in mind when negotiating a contract with prospective outsourcers due to the intimate nature of the relationship. Some issues to keep in mind are the accountability of performance, long-term flexibility, and confidentiality, and ethical issues. Partners should be held accountable for their performance, especially if it is an outsourced vendor. Usually, in strategic alliances or joint ventures, there is a sharing of the risks and rewards. Nevertheless, the organization should make sure that the work performed by the partner is up to their standards. The partner should provide an arrangement that builds in flexibility for the future in terms of variable capacity and variable pricing structure. Finally, confidentiality aspects of a company's information are addressed in all outsourcing contracts. To be effective, the outsourcer should be considered an extension of the organization. There must be confidence and trust that the partner will not share information with outsiders or reveal trade secrets.

A number of other issues are important as well. A thorough understanding and agreement by key management people of both companies on the objectives and ground rules for the alliance is a prerequisite for success. These discussions must deal with hard issues, such as who will be in charge of maintenance, coordination, and other functions. Also, a very well defined level of hierarchy within the organization to be shared between customer and service provider. Other issues must be resolved, such as which decisions will be made by each organization, which decisions must be approved by both companies, and how disputes should be resolved. If there are fundamental differences or too many minor differences between the two companies, the alliance should be re-examined.

There are many variations to any partnership agreement, and each arrangement is different depending on each partner's needs. The common denominator for all successful agreements is the willingness of each side to openly describe its requirements, both those that are essential and nonessential. A complete understanding of what each is expected to contribute and a realistic assessment of each party's ability to deliver is a prerequisite to a successful relationship. When maintenance contract scope become too exhaustive with very few exclusion, then listing exclusions in contracts under separate item brings clarity in scope.

Risks Review During Contract Negotiations

The following steps can aid Business managers (Service Provider) in reviewing and negotiating contracts:

Step 1: Evaluate the technical scope of services.

Consider whether the anticipated scope of services is within your firm's standard technical expertise to ensure your operations team can deliver, whether in-house or through subcontracting to a third party. Your team will also need to review the scope to ensure it is reasonable, clear and fully defined. Additionally, your operations team must have input on whether gray areas exist within the scope. For example, if it includes all "matters reasonably inferable from" the request for proposal, that may include tasks your team did not anticipate performing. If gray areas exist, your operations team may be able to request clarification from the client.

Step 2: Review the mobilization plan and activity schedule.

Assess whether the mobilization plan is reasonable. If your team is delayed in mobilization or completing the services, does the contract provide for damages? Understanding such concerns will help you craft the most reasonable schedule and contractual language possible to address any unique project risks.

Step 3: Review pricing and payment terms.

Understanding whether your client is the end client or somewhere in the middle will impact payment negotiations. Is your firm able to select its desired pricing structure and payment time frame? If not, can your team arrive at an acceptable agreement?

Step 4: Discuss the project location with politicaland location issues along with risks stemming from providing services there.

Either an internal travel management tool or a third-party vendor can provide updated research on potentially risky locations and practical advice on the risks, particularly if your firm is working abroad. The IT or security departments can also advise on any risks or challenges associated with working in a particular location.

Step 5: Assess your customer/client.

Do others vendors consider your client to be fair? In addition to your own industry knowledge, your firm can use a third-party vendor to research a potential client's history. If a client has a reputation for treating partners harshly, odds are someone in your industry knows about it and will share their knowledge if you ask.

Your team should assess whether the project is something your client normally handles or whether it is a new area or market. You must also decide if your firm is willing to work with a client who may expose your firm to rework or re-performance risk, refuse to pay in accordance with the terms of the contract, or generally be unpleasant to work for.

Step 6: Review the contract for your firm's "mandatory" provisions.

Mandatory provisions are those contractual terms and conditions that your firm views as especially important when reviewing and negotiating contracts. Depending on the client and the nature of the work, these provisions could include:

Scope, schedule and price. Ensure the proposed scope, schedule, price and payment terms are acceptable. Your operations team's input is crucial to assess whether any clarification or changes are needed.

Standard of care. Review the standard of care to ensure that it is reasonable. If your firm performs professional services, they cannot be "warranted," as this presents an insurability issue. Clients also often request that services be performed in accordance with the "highest degree of care." Consider whether your firm's insurance coverage will respond to a claim that is above your industry's normal standard of care. The answer is often "no" or "maybe not." If your client requires you to accept a higher standard of care, your operations team needs to understand the increased risk this places on project execution.

Limitation of liability. Whether the limitation of liability is to your firm's fee, a multiple of the fee, insurance required under the agreement or another mutually acceptable amount, including a limitation of liability helps define the total risk to your firm and your client. Public entities like federal clients, states, municipalities, cities and universities cannot include a limitation of liability in their contracts. In those cases, how will your firm mitigate the risk of potentially unlimited liability?

Waiver of consequential damages. A mutual waiver of consequential damages increases the likelihood of your firm's insurance responding to a claim. It also increases the likelihood that your client will work with you to mitigate damages.

Mutual indemnification. Both your firm and your client should indemnify each other for your own negligence. Like the limitation of liability, federal clients, states, municipalities, cities and universities cannot indemnify your firm. Your team should consider how likely it is that the client will behave negligently and cause damage to your firm.

Your firm may have additional contractual terms that it considers crucial to successful project execution. As the business manager, you should have relationships with your legal and operations teams that allow you to understand where those "pain points" are and what your firm wants to do about them. Keep in mind how hard of a line your firm is willing to take on these provisions. When would the firm be willing to walk away because a mandatory term is not included in the contract?

Step 7: Review the contract for "nice to have" provisions.

Nice to have provisions are terms that help your team manage risk but are not required, such as "notice of error" or the "opportunity to cure." Your team should consider whether the client will work with you to address and correct any mistakes you make during execution.

Many client contracts do not provide you with the opportunity to suspend services or terminate the agreement if your client breaches it. Your team should consider the likelihood that your client will breach the agreement in some way and, if it does, how you will want to respond.

Step 8: Review the contract for heightened risk provisions.

Some contract provisions can increase the risk to your firm. For example, performance guarantees and bonds are generally difficult for professional services firms to provide. If your client requires either, do they truly understand the nature of your services? If you agree to include either in a contract and your firm cannot meet it, are you now in breach of contract?

Another potential concern is the risk of liquidated damages, which are often related to schedule issues. If your operations team is delayed in providing a deliverable to the client, is your firm willing to be subject to potential liquidated damages to be paid daily until the delay is rectified?

The risk management team should also review any flow-down clauses from any of your client's clients. Often, when flow-downs are included, they take precedence over a conflicting term in your agreement with your client. This could negate much of your team's hard work in arriving at a reasonable standard of care, for example.

For the most part, the risks your team identifies during a preliminary review will not be deal-breakers. The risk management department will bring great value to the contract review and negotiation process by working with the operations team to identify and mitigate risks. Ultimately, it is about providing a solution to your internal clients that facilitates project execution while also protecting your firm from unreasonable risks.

Collaboration

After a partner has been selected, negotiating the partnering relationship begins to evolve. What distinguishes a partnering relationship from the traditional adversarial customer-suppler relationship? Apparently many purchasing agents think there is little difference. Unfortunately, the term "partnering" is frequently loosely used and abused. Often, partnerships are more "rhetoric than reality". For example, some would argue that a partnership exists when any type of long-term agreement is made between firms. However, agreements such as long-term contracts and special service arrangements do not have the type of commitment and cooperation needed to constitute a true partnership. These are contractual agreements, not partnerships. An even worse abuse of the term occurs when it is used to disguise a customer's attempt to control a service provider. Customers often say they want to be partners but continue to dominate the service provider. At least two characteristics distinguish true partnering relationships. First, partnering is a long-term relationship between the customer and the Service provider. Secondly, in partnering relationships, both parties have an interest in the other's well-being. Or more specifically, good partner relationships should have the following characteristics.

- The partners are proactive.
- The parties are integrating key processes and activities.
- There is a commitment to developing and maintaining cooperative and close relationships.

- There is a clear and well-structured framework for determining cost, price, and profit for both sides.

- A win-win philosophy exists.

- Both parties are committed to continuous improvement in all spheres of their activities.

The commitment and mutual dependency represented by these characteristics are what differentiate a partnership from a traditional adversarial approach to outsourcing.

The partnering relationship is normally initiated and established through the initial negotiations as previously discussed. Negotiation has been defined as "a process of potentially opportunistic interaction by which two or more parties, with some apparent conflict, seek to do better through jointly decided action then they could otherwise. This process is difficult and complicated when it is performed from the traditional simplistic an adversarial point of view. From a partnering perspective, things get even more complicated. In this case, each party has to be concerned with not only their own interests but also the interests of the other party as well.

In partnering, negotiation is a balance. Negotiating partnerships is a process of balancing conflict with cooperation, and relationship issues with substantive issues. In order to effect this balance and effect lasting relationships, customers and service providers need to consider both their cooperative and competitive positions, substantive issues and conduct a negotiation analysis.

Neither a purely cooperative nor a purely competitive perspective is appropriate when negotiating partnerships. The untrusting and adversarial win-lose nature of the purely competitive perspective obviously is not appropriate when entering a partnership. Conversely, choosing a purely cooperative perspective may compromise each party's self-interest. However, choosing an "enlightened self-interest" point of view balances the forces of cooperation and competition to effectively focus on mutual interests, merits, and results. This point of view recognizes that the needs of both parties must be satisfied, and thus recognizes that each party must work to ensure that the needs of both parties are met by the partnership.

Considering and including relationship issues in the negotiations is crucial. The traditional approach of focusing on substantive issues is a short-term outlook and focuses on short-term gains. However, long-term gains can only be obtained if negotiations consider the relationship. Relationship issues include establishing the procedures for interpersonal contacts, conflict resolution, teamwork, and procedures for monitoring the relationship's performance. Agreeing to such things upfront will put into place the mechanisms that will be used later to maintain and improve the relationship.

Conducting a negotiation analysis before interacting with the customer or supplier is also important. This analysis should include an examination of interests and issues; the generation of options; and an exploration of how options can be made into specific agreements. Examining the interests and issues involved is needed in order to determine each party's needs and their viable options. The generation of options is intuitively critical. As with any negotiation, each party must have at least more than one option. In partnerships, options are exceptionally important. When negotiating partnerships, the more viable options you have in mind entering the negotiation, the more likely you are going to be able to successfully match options with the other party.

Finally, when negotiating the partnership, and thereafter, the most important element of establishing and maintaining the relationship is trust. A trusting relationship exists when both the partners do the following.

- Do not act in a purely self-serving manner.
- Accurately disclose relevant information when requested.
- Not change the specifications for the product or service.
- Generally act in an ethical manner.

In conclusion, establishing and maintaining good partner relationships requires planning up-front, a balancing of needs, and an environment of trust.

Monitoring Service Provider Relationships

Once a partnership has been established and orders are being placed, it may be tempting to stop managing the process. After all, one of the reasons companies outsource is that they do not want to manage the maintenance process. Although outsourcing frees companies from the manpower resourcing and plant engineering/maintenance requirements of running a business, it does not free them from the need to monitor the relationship to ensure that it is satisfying the needs of both parties. A partnership must be managed and it is not possible to manage, without some kind of measurement. There are basically two methods and four elements of measuring partnership success and monitoring it.

Reporting Methods

- Reports prepared by the Service providers. i.e. Periodic reports daily report Monthly report, Annual report & specific event reports.
- Reports prepared by the customer

Interpersonal Methods

- Focus groups and strategy meetings
- Structured meeting between a customer and contractor representative on periodic/monthly basis
- Customer and service provider feedback

Measures of partnership performance must consider the complexity and unique nature of such relationships. Since each relationship is unique, so should be some of its performance measures. It is inappropriate to apply the same generic performance measures to all partners. When establishing performance measures, consideration should be given to the reasons the relationship was formed. Measures need to gauge how well the partnership is serving the purpose the partnership was established to serve, in the first place. Furthermore, while partnering relationships may be complex, their performance measures should not be. For performance measures of partnerships to be useful, they must be few, simple, and focus on what is really important.

Standard customer feedback form is usually the most commonly used tool, but the effectiveness of these instruments cannot be taken on face value, for reason well evident and needs no explanation.

Of the two parties, service providers are in the best position to provide new technology updates, equipment reports, Spare requirement, and returns. Obviously, in today's need for reduced inventories and speedy service, it is important to monitor the timeliness of the partnership. Suppliers can provide lead time reports that include order dates, promised dates, actual delivery dates, as well as the average lead time that resulted. If anything else can destroy a relationship it is money. Hence, a report listing invoiced prices, the price actually paid, and when such payments were received, will provide useful information. Another source of tension occurs when a service is not meeting the customer's needs. Likewise, the service provider is in the best position to provide reports summarizing customer returns and complaints.

On the other side of the partnership, the customer is in a uniquely qualified position to supply reports on the Spares procurement, Audit reports, Utility bills & other service reports on customer scope. Comparing the performance of the partnership with other suppliers can obviously yield good information as to the value of the relationship. Reports describing what products are being purchased, from which suppliers enable the service provider to work out total maintenance cost and cost per unit of production to find out the details to improvement.

A great deal of trust will be needed for this kind of information exchange, but in an effective partnership, it is mandatory.

Additionally, equipment failures/breakdowns and rework can provide telling information about how effectively the partners are communicating. When a customer rejects a service because of a cost or quality problem and the supplier reviews it holistically before justifying his action, the service provider is accepting the genuine reason as well. Hence, acceptance is an indication that both parties agree with what went wrong and what needs to be done to fix the problem. However, when a service provider rejects a customer's rejection, it is an indication that the parties have a different belief as to what constitutes a satisfactory product or service. Thus, a report describing supplier rejections can bring such communication breakdowns to light.

Focus groups can reveal opportunities for improvement in ways reports cannot. All the reports mentioned thus far can be used to bring to light exceptions to the normal delivery, pricing, and quality of the product or service. These exceptions can be used to fix problems that have already occurred. However, this method of monitoring is not designed to prevent problems before they occur. A less formal method is needed for this purpose. Periodic focus group meetings can be used to not only fix problems identified by the aforementioned reports but also to otherwise improve the partnership. These focus groups should consist of top management, as well as people within each organization that are a part of the partnership or a customer of the partnership. In such meetings, the partners can explore successful aspects of the relationship; potential areas for improvement; and innovative things that each party may be doing with other customers or suppliers.

Partners need to actively pursue feedback regarding the performance of the partnership. Often customers and service providers do not always give the feedback they could. Focus groups can be used for this purpose. But focus groups alone provide a relatively narrow sampling of viewpoints. Other methods can be used to solicit ideas for improvement. Random calls by buyers, account representatives, and top management to the other party can be used to get information regarding the performance of the relationship that would otherwise not be provided. Additionally, surveys sent to partners can be used to get an even broader representation of how the relationship is performing, and how it can be improved.

While it may be helpful to get numerous functions involved when monitoring the partnering relationships, ultimately someone needs to be accountable for ensuring that such monitoring takes place and that it is effective. For this reason, it is necessary to formally assign "relationship managers" for both partners. These relationship managers should work together to act as: focal points for the collection and dissemination of performance measures; a clearinghouse for daily problem resolution; and as owners of the monitoring process. In performing this function, these managers need to ensure that the benefits of the relationship are actively being measured and actively used to improve the relationship's performance.

As indicated, there are at least three constraints on the relationship. First, each partner brings certain fixed needs that must be fulfilled by the relationship. Secondly, each organization is going to have its own culture which will act as a constraint on the relationship. Lastly, there is a potentially illegal restraint of trade issues when customers and partners build relationships. These elements, along with the inputs described, all enter into the processes that result in the service cost, quality, and delivery. These outputs are evaluated, and the results are fed into corrective action procedures which act on the inputs and processes to improve the outputs. While this is obviously a simplified version of an extremely complex process, it does basically describe the elements of a partnering relationship. In order for this process to have any hope of succeeding, they must be implemented in consideration of both partner's needs, in an environment of mutual trust.

VIEWPOINT

- Warranty/Guarantee meaning has changed with time. Earlier it was the supplier trustworthiness of product performance with high factor of safety. In present industry in competitive environment, with more emphasis on optimization and process efficiency it is a statistics with cost of failure build in the price of remaining non-defective produced materials.

- Disclaimers/Limitation of liability etc. are the standard terms in contracts and different services. These to be used rarely, sensibly and in discretion only when becomes extremely necessary i.e. Job placement agency Investment advisors use these disclaimers to shield their non – performance. Posting opportunity to aspirant and advising investment as contractual commitment without looking, if they are relevant or serve any objective. Doing job without accountability doesn't seems to be good business idea. Service provider to develop synergy with customer and contribute considerably to make his business successful, rather than limiting to written guidelines. This is about going beyond obvious.

Chapter 5

Maintenance Organization

"An organization's ability to learn, and translate that learning into action rapidly, is the ultimate competitive advantage"

— Jack Welch

Organizing is the process of arranging resources (people, materials, technology, etc.) together to achieve the organization's strategies and goals. The way in which the various parts of an organization are formally arranged is referred to as the organization structure. It is a system involving the interaction of inputs and outputs. It is characterized by task assignments, workflow, reporting relationships, and communication channels that link together the work of diverse individuals and groups. Any structure must allocate tasks through a division of labor and facilitate the coordination of the performance results. Nevertheless, we have to admit that there is no one best structure that meets the needs of all circumstances. Organizational structures should be viewed as dynamic entities that continuously evolve to respond to changes in technology, processes, and environment.

Frederick W. Taylor introduced the concept of scientific management (time study and division of labor), while Frank and Lilian Gilbreth founded the concept of modern motion study techniques. The contributions of Taylor and the Gilbreths are considered as the basis for modern organization management until the middle of the twentieth-century maintenance has been carried out in an unplanned reactive way and for a long time, it has lagged behind other areas of industrial management in the application of formal techniques and/or information technology. With the realization of the impact of poor maintenance on enterprises' profitability, many managers are revising the organization of maintenance and have developed new approaches that foster effective maintenance organization.

Maintenance costs can be a significant factor in an organization's profitability. So, contemporary management considers maintenance as an integral function in achieving productive operations and high-quality products, while maintaining satisfactory equipment and machines reliability as demanded by the era of automation, flexible manufacturing systems (FMS), "lean manufacturing", and "just-in-time" operations.

However, there is no universally accepted methodology for designing maintenance systems, i.e., no fully structured approach leading to an optimal maintenance system (i.e., an organizational structure with a defined hierarchy of authority and span of control; defined maintenance procedures and policies, etc.). Identical product organizations, but different in technology advancement and production size, may apply different maintenance systems and the different systems may run successfully. So, maintenance systems are designed using experience and judgment supported by a number of formal decision tools and techniques. Nevertheless, two vital considerations should be considered: a strategy that decides on which level within the plant to perform maintenance, and hence outlining a structure that will support the maintenance; planning that handles day-to-day decisions on what maintenance tasks to perform and providing the resources to undertake these tasks.

The maintenance organizing function can be viewed as one of the basic and integral parts of the maintenance management function (MMF). The MMF consists of planning, organizing, implementing, and controlling maintenance activities. The management organizes, provides resources (personnel, capital, assets, material, and hardware, etc.) and leads to performing tasks and accomplishing targets. Once the plans are created, the management's task is to ensure that they are carried out in an effective and efficient manner. Having a clear mission, strategy, and objectives facilitated by corporate culture, organizing starts the process of implementation by clarifying job and working relations (chain of command, span of control, a delegation of authority, etc.).

In designing the maintenance organization there are important determinants that must be considered. The determinants include the capacity of maintenance, centralization vs decentralization, and in-house maintenance vs outsourcing. A number of criteria can be used to design the maintenance organization. The criteria include clear roles and responsibilities, effective span of control, facilitation of good supervision and effective reporting, and minimization of costs.

Maintenance managers must have the capabilities to create a division of labor for maintenance tasks to be performed and then coordinate results to achieve a common purpose. Solving performance problems and capitalizing on opportunities could be attained through the selection of the right persons, with the appropriate capabilities, supported by continuous training and good incentive schemes, in order to achieve organizational success in terms of performance effectiveness and efficiency.

Maintenance Organization Objectives and Responsibility

A maintenance organization and its position in the plant/whole organization is heavily impacted by the following elements or factors:

- Type of business, e.g., whether it is high tech, labor-intensive, production or service;
- Objectives: may include profit maximization, increasing market share, and other social objectives;
- Size and structure of the organization;
- Culture of the organization; and
- Range of responsibility assigned to maintenance

Responsibility Assigned to Site in charge/Facility Manager

Planning – Setting performance objectives and developing decisions on how to achieve them.

Organizing – Creating structure setting tasks (Dividing up the work), arranging resources (forming maintenance crews and coordinating activities to perform maintenance tasks).

Implementing – Executing the plans to meet the set performance objective.

Controlling – Measuring performance of the maintained equipment and taking preventive and corrective actions to restore the desired (designed) specification.

Organizations seek one or several of the following objectives: profit maximization, specific quality level of service or products, minimizing costs, safe and clean environment, or human resource development. It is clear that all of these objectives are heavily impacted by maintenance and therefore the objectives of maintenance must be aligned with the objectives of the organization.

The principal responsibility of maintenance is to provide a service to enable an organization to achieve its objectives. The specific responsibilities vary from one organization to another; however, they generally include the following according to:

- Keeping assets and equipment in good condition, well configured and safe to perform their intended functions;

- Perform all maintenance activities including preventive, predictive; corrective, overhauls, design modification and emergency maintenance in an efficient and effective manner;

- Conserve and control the use of spare parts and material;

- Commissioning support in new plants and plant expansions; and

- Operate utilities and conserve energy.

The above responsibilities and objectives impact the organization structure for maintenance as will be shown in the coming sections.

Determinants of a Maintenance Organization

The maintenance organization's structure is determined after planning the maintenance capacity. The level of centralization or decentralization adopted heavily influences the maintenance capacity. In this section, the main issues that must be addressed when forming the maintenance organization's structure are presented. The issues are capacity planning, centralization vs decentralization, and in-house vs outsourcing.

Maintenance Capacity Planning

Maintenance capacity planning determines the required resources for maintenance including the required competency, administration, equipment, tools, and space to execute the maintenance load efficiently and meet the objectives of the maintenance department. Critical aspects of maintenance capacity are the numbers and skills of technicians required to execute the maintenance load. It is difficult to determine the exact number of various types of technician since the maintenance load is uncertain. Therefore accurate forecasts for the future maintenance work demand are essential for determining the maintenance capacity. In order to have better utilization of manpower, organizations tend to reduce the number of available technician below their expected needs. This is likely to result in a backlog of uncompleted maintenance work. This backlog can also be cleared when the maintenance load is less than the capacity. Making long run estimations is one of the areas in maintenance capacity planning that is both critical and not well developed in practice.

Centralization vs Decentralization

The decision to organize maintenance in a centralized, decentralized, or hybrid form depends largely on the organization is philosophy, maintenance load, size of the plant, and skills of technician. The advantages of centralization are:

1. Provides more flexibility and improves utilization of resources such as highly skilled services and special equipment and therefore results in more efficiency;

2. Allows more efficient line supervision;

3. Allows more effective on the job training; and

4. Permits the purchasing of modern equipment.

However, it has the following disadvantages:

5. Less utilization of specialized services since more time is required for getting to and from jobs;

6. Supervision of activity becomes more difficult and as such less maintenance control is achieved;

7. Less specialization on complex hardware is achieved since different persons work on the same hardware; and

8. More costs of transportation are incurred due to the remoteness of some of the maintenance work.

In a decentralized maintenance organization, departments are assigned to specific areas or units. This tends to reduce the flexibility of the maintenance system as a whole. The range of skills available becomes reduced and manpower utilization is usually less efficient than in centralized maintenance. In some cases, a compromise solution that combines centralization and decentralization is better. This type of hybrid is called a cascade system. The cascade system organizes maintenance in areas and whatever exceeds the capacity of each area is challenged to a centralized unit. In this fashion, the advantages of both systems may be reaped.

In-house vs Outsourcing

At this level, management considers the sources for building the maintenance capacity. The main sources or options available are in-house by direct hiring, outsourcing, or a combination of in-house and outsourcing. The criteria for selecting sources for building and maintaining maintenance capacity include strategic considerations, technological and economic factors. The following are criteria that can be employed to select among sources for maintenance capacity:

1. Availability and dependability of the source on a long term basis;

2. The capability of the source to achieve the objectives set for maintenance by the organization and its ability to carry out the maintenance tasks;

3. Short term and long term costs;

4. Organizational secrecy in some cases may be subjected to leakage;

5. Long term impact on maintenance personnel expertise; and

6. A special agreement by manufacturer or regulatory bodies that set certain specifications for

Maintenance and Environmental Emissions

Examples of maintenance tasks which could be outsourced are:

- Work for which the skill of specialists is required on a routine basis and which is readily available in the market on a competitive basis, e.g.,

- Installation and periodic inspection and repair of automatic fire sprinkler systems;

- Inspection and repair of air conditioning systems;

- Inspection and repair of heating systems; and

- Inspection and repair of Electrical System, IT network etc.

- When it is cheaper than recruiting your own staff and accessible at a short notice of time.

The issues and criteria presented in the above section may help organizations in designing or re-designing their maintenance organization.

Design of the Maintenance Organization

A maintenance organization is subjected to frequent changes due to uncertainty and desire for excellence in maintenance. Maintenance and plant managers are always swinging from supporters of centralized maintenance to decentralized ones, and back again. The result of this frequent change is the creation of responsibility channels and direction of the new organization's accomplishments vs the accomplishments of the former structure. So, the service team have to adjust to the new roles. To establish a maintenance organization an objective method that caters for factors that influence the effectiveness of the organization is needed.

Competencies and continuous improvement should be the driving considerations behind an organization's design and re-design.

Current Criteria for Organizational Change

Many organizations were re-designed to fix a perceived problem. This approach in many cases may raise more issues than solve the specific problem.

Among the reasons to change a specific maintenance organization's design are:

1. Dissatisfaction with maintenance performance by the organization or plant management;

2. A desire for increased accountability;

3. A desire to minimize manufacturing costs, so maintenance resources are moved to report to a production supervisor, thereby eliminating the (perceived) need for the maintenance supervisor;

4. Many plant managers are frustrated that maintenance seems slow-paced, that is, every job requires excessive time to get done. Maintenance people fail to understand the business of manufacturing, and don't seem to be part of the team. This failure results in decentralization or distribution of maintenance resources between production units; and

5. Maintenance costs seem to rise remarkably, so more and more contractors are brought in for larger jobs that used to get done in-house.

Criteria to Assess Organizational Effectiveness

Rather than designing the organization to solve a specific problem, it is more important to establish a set of criteria to identify an effective organization. The following could be considered as the most important criteria:

6. Roles and responsibilities are clearly defined and assigned;

7. The organization puts maintenance in the right place in the organization;

8. The flow of information is both from top-down and bottom-up;

9. The span of control is effective and supported with well trained personal;

10. Maintenance work is effectively controlled;

11. Continuous improvement is built in the structure;

12. Maintenance costs are minimized; and

13. Motivation and organization culture.

Basic Types of Organizational Models

To provide consistently the capabilities listed above we have to consider three types of organizational designs.

- Centralized maintenance. All Service expertise and related maintenance functions report to a central maintenance manager. The strengths of this structure are: allows economies of scale; enables in-depth skill development; and enables departments (i.e., a maintenance department) to accomplish their functional goals (not the overall organizational goals). This structure is best suited for small to medium-size organizations. The weaknesses of this structure are: it has a slow response time to environmental changes; may cause delays in decision making and hence longer response time; leads to poor horizontal coordination among departments and involves a restricted view of organizational goals.

- Decentralized maintenance. All Service expertise and maintenance function support staff report to operations or area maintenance. The strengths of this structure are that it allows the organization to achieve adaptability and coordination in production units and efficiency in a centralized overhaul group and it facilitates effective coordination both within and between maintenance and other departments. The weaknesses of this structure are that it has the potential for excessive administrative overheads and may lead to conflict between departments.

- Matrix structure, a form of a hybrid structure. Service expertise are allocated in some proportion to production units or area maintenance and to a central maintenance function that supports the whole plant or organization. The strengths of this matrix structure are: it allows the organization to achieve coordination necessary to meet dual demands from the environment and flexible sharing of human resources. The weaknesses of this structure are: it causes maintenance employees to experience dual authority which can be frustrating and confusing; it is time-consuming and requires frequent meetings and conflict resolution sessions. To remedy the weaknesses of this structure management with good interpersonal skills and extensive training is required.

Material and Spare Parts Management

The responsibility of this unit is to ensure the availability of material and spare parts in the right quality and quantity at the right time at the minimum cost. In large or medium-size organizations this unit may be independent of the maintenance organization; however, in many circumstances, it is part of maintenance. It is a service that supports maintenance programs. Its effectiveness depends to a large extent on the standards maintained within the store's system. The duties of material and spare parts unit include:

1. Develop in coordination with maintenance effective stocking polices to minimize ordering, holding and shortages costs;
2. Coordinate effectively with suppliers to maximize organization benefits;
3. Keep good inward, receiving, and safekeeping of all supplies;
4. Issue materials and supplies;
5. Maintain and update records; and
6. Keep the stores orderly and clean.

Establishment of Authority and Reporting

Overall administrative control usually rests with the maintenance department, with its head reporting to top management. This responsibility may be delegated within the maintenance establishment. The relationships and responsibility of each maintenance division/section must be clearly specified together with the reporting channels. Each job title must have a job description prescribing the qualifications and the experience needed for the job, in addition to the reporting channels for the job.

Quality of Leadership and Supervision

The organization, procedures, and practices instituted to regulate the maintenance activities and demands in an industrial undertaking are not in themselves a guarantee of satisfactory results. The senior executive and his staff must influence the whole functional activity. Maintenance performance can never rise above the quality of its leadership and supervision. Good leadership stems the team-work which is the essence of success in any enterprise. Talent and ability must be recognized and fostered; good work must be noticed and commended; and carelessness must be exposed and addressed.

Incentives

The varied nature of the maintenance tasks, and differing needs and conditions arising, together with the influence of production activity, are not attuned to the adoption of incentive systems of payment. There are, however, some directions in which incentive applications can be usefully considered. One obvious case is that of repetitive work. The forward planning of maintenance work can sometimes lead to an incentive payment arrangement, based on the completion of known tasks in a given period, but care must be taken to ensure that the required standards of work are not compromised. In some case, maintenance incentives can be included in output bonus schemes, by arranging that continuity of production, and attainment of targets provides rewards to both production and maintenance personnel.

Education and Training

Nowadays it is also recognized that the employers should not only select and place personnel, but should promote schemes and provide facilities for their further education and training, so as to increase individual proficiency, and provide recruits for the supervisory and senior grades. For senior staff, refresher courses comprise lectures on specific aspects of their work; they also encourage the interchange of ideas and discussion.

The further education of technical grades, craft workers, and apprentices is usually achieved through joint schemes, sponsored by employers in conjunction with the local education authority. Employees should be encouraged to take advantage of these schemes, to improve proficiency and promotion prospects.

A normal trade background is often inadequate to cope with the continuing developments in technology. The increasing complexity and importance of maintenance engineering warrants a marked increase in training of machine operators and maintenance craftsmen through formal school courses, reinforced by informed instruction by experienced supervisors. The organization must have a well-defined training program for each employee.

The following provides guidelines for developing and assessing the effectiveness of the training program:

1. Evaluate current personnel performance;
2. Assess training needs analysis;
3. Design the training program;
4. Implement the program; and
5. Evaluate program effectiveness.

The evaluation is done either through a certification program or by assessing the ability to achieve desired performance by persons who have taken a particular training program. The implementation of the above five steps provides the organization with a framework to motivate personnel and improve performance.

Management and Labor Relations

The success of an undertaking depends significantly on the care taken to form a community of well-informed, keen, and lively people working harmoniously together. Participation creates satisfaction and necessary team spirit. In modern industry, quality of work-life (QWL) programs have been applied with considerable success, in the form of management conferences, work councils, quality circles, and joint conferences identified with the activities. The joint activities help the organization more fully achieve its purposes.

Maintenance Outsourced

Once the owner decides to outsource the maintenance functions of the Maintenance organization complement and integrate with the customer maintenance organization as per agreed contract with well-defined boundaries and appropriate overlap to form seamless co-operation without any service interruption. Here also service partners can have a different option in form of centralized control or decentralized control depending upon the number of sites in operation and competency distribution across them.

Organization at Site

The different customer from vide industry may demand different manpower deployment plan as per there requirement. The deputed manpower can be broadly characterized in subgroups irrespective of their position as organization structure-

The three broad levels shall be characterized as hereunder;

1. Initiator/Driver (Approx. 10% of Site team) – These comprise of Site In-charge, Area in charge, and any other team member on the discretion of site In charge. In addition to the normal site assigned

responsibility, they shall actively identify new potential ideas from within the team and other available resources via different brainstorming session. These Ideas can be Kaizen, Energy-saving plan, Equipment modification, safety, etc. They will make its final presentation with resource requirements and expected outcomes with a comparison of existing status. Once the final plan is worked out with drawings and necessary resources, the same to be discussed with the customer and approved by the customer.

2. Moderator (Approx. 20-30% of Site Team) – Once Modification/Improvement plan is approved and resources arranged than the modification is executed under the guidance of Initiator with a series of trials. These trial results are recorded for different variable conditions with a comparison with past references. The benefit whatsoever should be quantified in quality and quantity.

3. Executor (Approx. 70-60%) – These are the main part of the team, executing ideas on site. They are responsible for sustaining the plan, once validated by the moderator. Moderator continues to supervise the same to sustain the desired results.

The proportion of different categories (quantity and qualitatively marked) are just indicative and are subject to variation depending upon Industry type, customer requirement, Manpower deployment plan, etc.

Value Addition vs Value Edition

Value addition is the buzzword very popular in the outsourcing business, justifying the premium price. Any value addition attempt once validated by management to be executed and benefits to be monitored pertaining to sustainable benefits else wise in an attempt of implementing too many suggestions without proper thoughts appears to be Value Edition instead of Value addition. Value edition is a temporary process and manipulated value addition, may be value addition in one dimension causing value reduction in another dimension. i.e. reducing power consumption by stopping part of equipment affecting the quality of the product.

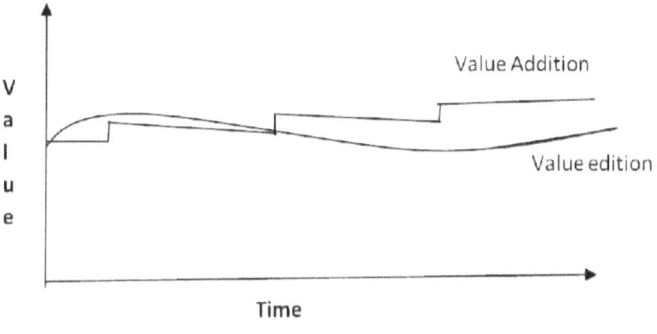

Fig – VI

The above picture clearly depicts the difference between value addition and value edition. Value addition is really useful if sustained with quantified impact validated annually.

Checklist as Value addition – Adding a new checklist or a few additional points in the checklist is normally followed trend in the industry as value addition. Although checklist has emerged as a trend from maybe critical services like aircrafts in air force. As it is extremely essential to check all points thoroughly before flight take-offs as anything missed out by whatever small proportion shall cost heavily in terms of equipment cost, human life, training, and other associated costs. No doubt, on the importance of checklist in maintenance as it is necessary, but overdoing of it may not yield the desired result but add on indirect cost and inefficiencies. Checklist to be reviewed periodically and revised with the addition or deletion of activity or frequency looking into criticality and cost.

Similarly, filling the same checklist on a digital instrument like tab or mobile apps instead of on paper is only an eyewash and in no way going to add value except saving the environment by discouraging the use of paper. This digital checklist can be effective if variables/parameters can be changed on basis of rating and type of equipment. Moreover, the use of different regression techniques (Linear or logistic) can be incorporated to calculate instantaneously the residual life or de-rating characteristic shall make the process more fruitful.

General scope of supply for Maintenance Contractor

Maintenance responsibility in any organization remains similar as discussed in the initial part of the chapter. However, the scope of total activities is distributed between the Owner and contractor with a well-defined responsibility matrix in place. However, in general, maintenance service provider responsibilities can be elaborated as:

Deployment of shift and general shift manpower – This is the basic requirement of such contracts. The deployed team may include – Engineer, Supervisor, Technician, Helper with quantity, and competency level required by customer or assessment done by service provider looking into the work scope and KPI undertaken. The service provider is responsible for his people as follows-

1. Selection of competent employees and offering them a position in their payroll or outsource to other service providers.

   - Taking care of employee attrition

   - Calculating emoluments and timely disbursement of the same along with other compliance requirements.

   - Arranging facility logistics i.e. Vehicle for site commuting, Guesthouse, etc.

2. Supply of tools, PPE & consumables

3. Supply of spares and/or inventory management.

4. Plant safety, Energy Audits and Other audits to evaluate the plant condition on a periodic basis.

Manpower Deployment Plan: Manpower deployment remains a key issue in any maintenance contract and varies for different industries, customers, regions, contract types, etc.

In case of a new Greenfield, project coming up for operation, the prime requirement lies with identifying the competent manpower arranging logistics and infrastructure without much of reference and imbibing into the organization culture. Whereas for changing up the contract or switching in-house activities to outsource service offers altogether different challenges and needs to be handled sensibly with responsibility and may emerge as plant strategy from top management.

Most of the time in the situation of change of service provider customer compels a new vendor to continue with a major part of an existing team, which may be an initial advantage for both customer and contractor in term of a smooth transition. The transition here means only about the activities, not the work culture or ethics. But it implies unfairness on the contractor part, who has superseded the existing contractor with the promise of better delivery. Better delivery with the same setup is if not difficult, but is time-consuming. Which can be somewhere from 3 months to a year. If this is a must activity as a strategy from the customer side, to be spelled out clearly in contract with exact no. of people with their competency matrix in the tender document.

Site mobilization for any new plant within the agreed period is a challenge for any contractor. Site mobilization can be in one time or in stages as per the contractor's capabilities.

Service Model and People

People are an important ingredient in-service model; as it may not be that you have hired a complete team of people who just didn't get it. Maybe you have designed a service model for Superman Employees which you wish you had, but you actually don't or not affordable at existing contract value.

It is difficult to Design a service model that allows average employees, not just the exceptional ones to produce service excellence as an everyday routine. It requires lots of motivation, training, and teamwork forming the basis of the great service organization. First and foremost thing for manpower deployment is about knowing customer-

1. Find what your customer values first.

2. Service is more about best in class customer interaction.

3. Employees' best of the best in both Attitude and aptitude are expensive.

4. People with a good attitude are desired in the service industry.

5. Emphasize training and develop centralized expert service to deal with any problem at the earliest arising of less aptitude of the employees.

6. Expert Services (In house/External) can be provided as per requirement for the responsive customer and offered to utilize ideal hrs. ("Happy Hrs.") for less responsive to the budget customer with high – efficiency requirements across the spectrum. Successful Employee management system.

Successful Employee management system

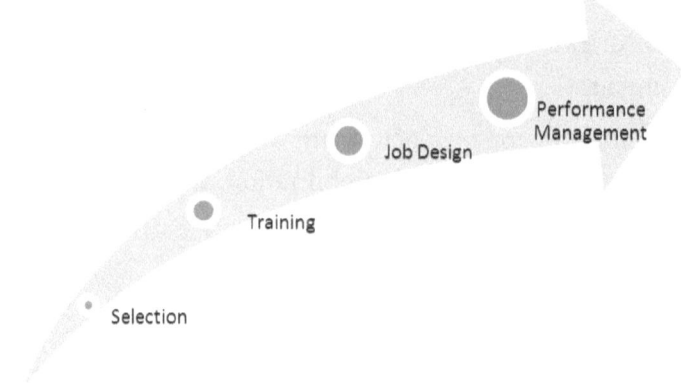

Typical Organogram with *duty post, for any industry as in any proposal/ contract is as under –

Shift	Site In – charge	Electrical Supervisor	Mechanical Supervisor	Electrician	Fore man	Total
Gen	1	1	1	2		5
Shift A				1	1	2
Shift B				1		1
Shift C				1	1	2
Total	1	1	1	5	2	10

- Duty post means active position on routine and it is usually in addition to off & leave reliever.

- Qualification and experience criteria for each position are specifically maintained in separate profile matrix in contract.

The most of the successful service models incorporate a mechanism for pricing differentiation on premium and discount offering.

Ways to Invoice for excellence

- Charge Customer extra for it – in a palatable way.

- Make cost reductions that also improve service.

- Make service improvement that also reduces cost.

Writing Job Descriptions

Job descriptions are important for ensuring the link between the Competency required and the functions performed by staff. Job descriptions can be improved or updated by linking them to either the generic or a customized one.

In the case of an existing job description, one approach is to indicate which units or elements of competence are applicable by adding a list of the relevant titles.

In the case of a new job description, the units of competence can serve as a useful prompt in deciding the nature and scope of responsibilities.

The sphere of influence and complexity of an organisation will impact the requirements for maintenance management. The entity's job grading system and the assessment of job descriptions evaluate both spheres of influence and complexity and associate that with the identification of qualification and experience required.

Linking organogram titles to job descriptions can:

- Help ensure job descriptions for maintenance management staff are complementary and line up with maintenance management plan and objectives;

- facilitate the process of developing new job descriptions and revising existing job descriptions; and

- enable the management and development needs of the job holder to be defined and planned with some precision.

Planning Recruitment and Selection

The starting point for effective recruitment and selection is ensuring that the requirements of the job to be filled are explicit and up to date. As described above, the framework provides a useful tool to support the development and review of job descriptions. In particular, when job descriptions are linked to the relevant units, these units will contain a description of the skills, behaviors, knowledge, and understanding required for competent performance.

This provides a useful indication of the attributes of the ideal candidate for the job (that is, the basis of a person's specification). In this way, the framework can be used to support the development of accurate and up-to-date job descriptions and person specifications, which are the foundation of effective recruitment and selection.

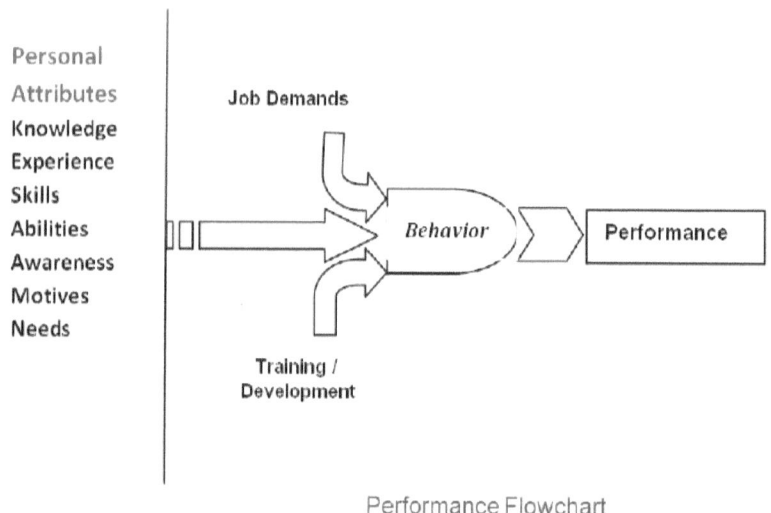

Performance Flowchart

Fig-VII

Developing Role Profiles

Role profiles differ from job descriptions in that they describe what the organisation should expect from everyone with a particular level of responsibility or experience: for example, Asset Head or Maintenance Management Planner. Job descriptions focus on what is expected of individuals with different levels of responsibility within a role.

Role profiles are a useful tool for ensuring that the structure of roles and responsibilities within an organisation are consistent with what the organisation is trying to achieve.

In developing role profiles for maintenance management, the first task is to define the structure of roles and responsibilities necessary to deliver the maintenance management plan and objectives. The second task is to define the levels of competence and responsibility needed to fulfill these roles and ensure there are healthy development paths between them.

Identifying Learning and Development Need

When job descriptions have been linked to the framework, job holders or their employers can review the units relevant to their job, to assess where they are currently competent and where they may require further learning and development.

This process of identifying learning and development needs may take place in a variety of contexts, from informal (e.g. self – assessment) through to more formal processes (e.g. supervision and appraisal).

A job holder and his/her line manager may agree to review the required skills, knowledge, and understanding from selected units. This provides an objective standard against which to judge the job holder's existing skills, knowledge, and understanding and to identify and prioritize training and development needs.

In this way, the framework can be used to identify and prioritize learning and development needs and recognize existing competences, knowledge, and understanding.

Competency Mapping

Competency Mapping is the process of identifying the gap between required skill and available skill to execute a job and design a process to bridge the gap.

A competency can be explained as a mix of skills, related knowledge and attributes to produce a job/task to a set standard. A competency standard can be described as a generally accepted standard or specification of performance which sets out the skills, knowledge, and attitudes required to operate effectively.

Understanding the competencies to employees acts bilaterally, the organization will empower employees to take charge of their careers; direct their own personal development, and continually self-evaluate and improve and organization also use the information to assign the right person a right job.

This Maintenance Management, establishes competencies according to the following format:

- Competency title: The short term used for the competency, such as Site Incharge, Electrical Supervisor, etc.

- Behaviour at a competent level: What the person shows when displaying the competency. It is a behavior that an observer can see or expect to see. The behavioral indicators integrate the knowledge, skills, and attributes components of competencies so that they make the competency come "alive" in the context of how the job is performed.

A set of competency standards for employees outlining the expected knowledge, skills, and attributes of employees explicit for those within and outside the organisation. When implemented properly a competency mapping can:

i. Create a common language for human resource interventions, as all interventions are according to the same competency framework and requirement aligned with the contract agreement.

ii. Translate the organization's vision and goals into expected employee behavior, as the desired behavior is known to all employees, and training intervention is designed accordingly.

iii. Implement more effective and legally compliant recruitment, selection, and assessment methods, as the requirements are appropriately defined and can, therefore be measured accordingly by utilising different selection methods. The competencies define the requirements for success in a particular role and it can become the selection criteria.

iv. Provide a benchmark against which individuals can be evaluated for recruitment and selection, performance management, and succession planning. Since the required competency standard can be defined clearly upfront, it can also assist with reducing subjectivity in performance appraisals.

v. Identify areas for employee development that are directly linked to desired outcomes and organizational objectives. The same competencies become the basis for making decisions about employees' development needs;

vi. Target training costs in areas that will realize the most return on investment; and

vii. identify gaps between present skill sets and future requirements to assist with the management of succession. It can assist with identifying development needs for various levels at different site locations and identifying pools of appropriate people that could fill those positions in the future.

This competency/skill inventory to be formulated centrally and used for future deployment for catering requirements for new upcoming sites and addressing attrition issues for existing site contracts. It will be encouraging to provide a conducive environment for employees to develop competency in the areas of their interest.

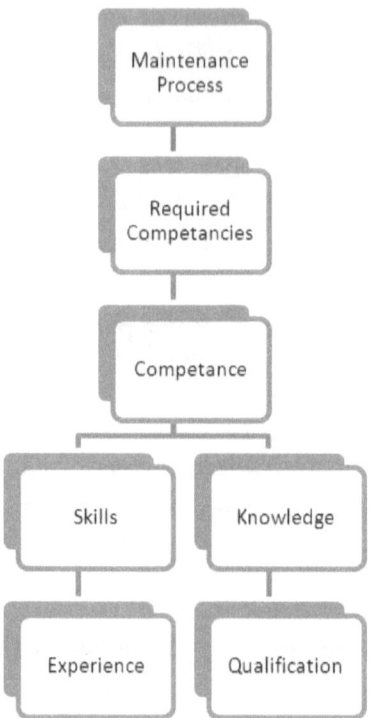

Typical maintenance competency requirement: This is the brief structure of some of the general maintenance competency and shall vary with site, Industry, Equipment population, and other plant parameters.

Typical Maintenace Competancies (Sample)	
Competency	**Description**
Align maintenance plan with organisational plan.	Integration of organisation plans; planning maintenance and setting maintenance objectives and goals while ensuring that maintenance, lifecycle, Human resources, procurement and logistic plans align with organisational and asset management plans.
Collate documentation and determine facility component	Interpretation of codes of practice: Understanding and knowledge regarding the technical standards and legislation that include processes for the identification, acceptable updating and compliance assurance of standards and legislation in the asset management context. The development of specifications and measurement of delivery against specifications

Analyse Equipment criticalityupto component level and determine the impact and likelihood of failure	Conducting FMCEA, Lifecycle analysis: Analysing, interpreting and balancing the costs and benefits of different maintenance activities of various assets.
Assess the condition and determine the reliability of components.	Condition/reliability assessment: Execution of processes and activities used by an organisation to assess the performance and health of its assets. Reliability engineering: Ensuring that an item shall operate to a defined standard for a defined period of time in a defined environment based on reliability analysis techniques
Scheduling Work and resource planning.	Cost estimating: Interpreting information and estimating the cost for short, medium and longer terms on all assets and services related to the maintenance of assets. Planning and organising: Planning and organising the work of the work unit and groups, using goal setting, objectives, targets, creating work schedules and work plans with associated budgets and resources, according to the organisation's procedures, in order to achieve the tasks, functions and results/outputs required of the work unit.
Condition monitoring and testing different components	Testing components and applying technology on maintenance diagnostic systems: Using technology in maintenance management systems to support the decision-making processes in accordance with the maintenance management plan.
Record Maintenance calls and determine maintenance actions.	Execution of administrative activities and procedures for the operation of an office or facility through organising and scheduling events, record keeping and effective communication with stakeholders. Risk assessment and monitoring: Identifying, quantifying and mitigating risk and exploiting opportunities.

Continued…

Analysing historic maintenance information.	Reliability engineering: Ensuring that an item shall operate to a defined standard for a defined period of time in a defined environment based on reliability analysis techniques
Planning Shutdown or outage Including demand management and prepare job cards	The process involves identifying an asset into its major elements of Process/System. components with useful life are: different Equipment assemblies & subassemblies, heating and ventilating and cooling system, electrical and lighting system, fire protection, plumbing system, elevator system, fixed equipment assets and IT infrastructure. Interpretation of codes of practice: Understanding and knowledge regarding the technical standards and legislation that include processes for the identification, acceptable updating and compliance assurance of standards and legislation in the asset management context. The development of specifications and measurement of delivery against specifications. Planning and organising: Planning and organising the work of the work unit and groups, using goal setting, objectives, targets, creating work schedules and work plans with associated budgets and resources, according to the organisation's procedures, in order to achieve the tasks, functions and results/outputs required of the work unit.
Safety, Health and Enviornment	Understanding and knowledge regarding the technical standards and legislation that include processes for the identification, acceptable updating and compliance assurance of standards and legislation in the asset management context. The development of specifications and measurement of delivery against specifications.

Re – assembling and commissioning after shutdown or outage.	Planning and organising the work of the work unit and groups, using goal setting, objectives, targets, creating work schedules and work plans with associated budgets and resources, according to the organisation's procedures, in order to achieve the tasks, functions and results/outputs required of the work unit. Asset operations: Asset operations is concerned with processes that provide instructions to operators about how to operate the asset with the appropriate design, maintenance, and operational parameters. This includes the development of an asset operations strategy and plans that outline the approach, activities and resources involved in managing and implementing operations.
Manage Faults and incidents	The management of faults and incidents in a systematic manner. This includes determining the likelihood of failure, fault analysis, use of standard responses, temporary and permanent repairs as well as the taking over and handing back of sites.
Maintenance record management	Execution of administrative activities and procedures for the operation of an office or facility through organising and scheduling events, record keeping and effective communication with stakeholders.
Monitoring maintenance actions implemented against the maintenance plan: • Monthly reporting against the maintenance plan. • Quarterly performance reviews; and • Analysing and planning corrective action.	Evaluating, identifying and using appropriate technologies in the workplace in order to enhance productivity, efficiency, responsiveness and the quality of service provided in order to aid the achievement of the organisation's goals and objectives. Monitoring and overseeing the performance of systems and staff. Project Management: Planning and managing projects by creating work breakdown schedules (WBS), activity schedules, time scales and timelines with associated budgets in order to deliver projects on time, within cost and at the required quality level

Continued…

Knowledge management	Measuring and improving or upgrading of work methods, procedures and systems and decreasing costs in order to improve the quality and cost efficiency of services and products delivered to clients
Maintenance Management System	Applying technology on maintenance management systems: Evaluating, identifying and using appropriate technologies in the workplace in order to enhance productivity, efficiency, responsiveness and the quality of service provided in order to aid the achievement of the organisation's goals and objectives. Monitoring and overseeing the performance of systems and staff.
Assessing the current stage of maintenance management performance	Evaluating, identifying and using appropriate technologies in the workplace in order to enhance productivity, efficiency, responsiveness and the quality of service provided in order to aid the achievement of the organisation's goals and objectives. Monitoring and overseeing the performance of systems and staff. Mentoring and professional development: Developing and coaching others and constructively reviewing the work of others in order to improve and advance the skills, knowledge and performance levels of those who report to them.
Developing performance improvement targets.	Performance Improvement: Evaluating, identifying and using appropriate technologies in the workplace in order to enhance productivity, efficiency, responsiveness and the quality of service provided in order to aid the achievement of the organisation's goals and objectives. Monitoring and overseeing the performance of systems and staff.

Competancy Matching: Once the gaps have been identified, the maintenance planning function should compile a strategy to address the gap through training, recruitment, and other human resource development processes. Once it has been customised to meet the requirements of an organisation, the Maintenance Management Competency Framework can underpin a systematic approach to gaining assurance that people working in maintenance management are competent to fulfill their roles and responsibilities.

Training: Whether training is of generic form or customized, the knowledge and understanding requirements can be used in designing and planning education programmes, training courses and other development activities. In planning or designing a learning programme, it is useful to subdivide the relevant knowledge and understanding into the following categories:

- General knowledge and understanding including contract management; – *Within scope of this book*

- Industry or sector-specific knowledge and understanding; and

- organization and context-specific knowledge and understanding.

The competency mapping provides a basis for discussing and agreeing personal learning objectives and the evidence that is needed to demonstrate achievement of these.

The skill upgrading programs also provides an objective benchmark against which to evaluate the impact of organizational learning and development activities along with enhanced customer satisfaction.

Supply Chain Management

Supply-chain management is proactive and involves the optimization of the flow of information, materials and payment between the supplier and the maintenance-contracting firm. The objective is to construct an integrated supply chain that uses supplier expertise, capabilities and technology in order to reduce costs and improve service/maintenance capability.

Traditionally, the maintenance outsourcing firm has viewed procurement as a disconnected process involving the movement of information, material and payment across a series of independent and autonomous internal and external organizational boundaries. The challenge for the company is to manage its supply chain and forge these autonomous entities into a continuous value chain that starts with the request for information or quotation and continues flawlessly during entire cycle of contract. Managing the supply chain can reduce costs, increase productivity and improve quality, which will make the maintenance outsourcing firm more competitive and increase customer satisfaction.

Developing a successful and effective supply chain is not easy. The complexity in case of maintenance contractor is somewhat more complex and subject to larger uncertainty. Start slow and with manageable objectives. Define the client value. Work with unique and qualified first tier connections. Make sure to involve the project design teams. Focus on managed costs. Mobilize the chain.

Maintenance Repair and Operating Supplies (MRO)

MRO (maintenance, repair, and operating supply) items are supplies utilized in the production process, that is not ultimately seen in the end products themselves. MRO items may include:

- Pay roll agency for HR function (In case major site deployment are on subcontract)
- Other service & OEM vendors
- Training Partners
- PPE
- Site Infrastructure &Computers
- Industrial equipment/Spares i.e. valves, compressors, pumps(As agreed in contract)
- Consumables (cleaning, laboratory, and office supplies)
- Plant upkeep supplies (lubricants, gaskets, repair tools)
- Periodic/Specialist Services
- Other vendors for transportation etc.

Many people don't fully appreciate the vital role MRO items play in keeping supply chains running smoothly. But failure to routinely maintain, repair, and overhaul systems, can cripple a business. Contrarily, businesses that diligently maintain MRO inventory and optimize supply chains, can better supply products to customers in a timely and economical manner.

But a dedicated supply chain professional can remedy this, by tracking the following:

- Full lists of required MRO items generally used
- Lead times needed to resupply MRO items
- MRO item usage and depletion rates

Strategic Sourcing

A supply chain professional can strategically manage MRO supplies by learning where to source materials economically. It may require cultivating multiple relationships, depending on the nature of the MRO supplies--be they for regulatory, engineering, safety, or other purposes. Certain suppliers focus in some areas, but not others.

MRO costs should be negotiated annually, to keep costs down. Consolidating MRO suppliers, when possible, also makes good fiscal sense, as shaving even just a few percentage points from an MRO budget can radically improve a company's bottom line. On the other hand, failure to properly inventory a supply chain with necessary MRO items can result in production shut-downs and slow-downs, diminished product availability, and ultimately customer attrition.

Today's supply chains are increasingly complex, making a data-driven approach to supply chain management a must. Data-driven SCM provides visibility from end to end for monitoring the flow of information, services and goods from procurement and delivery to the end consumer. Data isn't the only driver of effective supply chain management; other factors such as good vendor and supplier relationships, effective cost control, securing the right logistics partners and adopting innovative supply chain technologies make a big impact, too.

Supply chain optimization isn't a simple undertaking, but effective SCM offers numerous benefits that improve the bottom line. Here's a look at few of the most important benefits of effective supply chain management. Success of supply chain depends upon its alignment with customer priority.

Eg. In a newly mobilized site, where customers insisting on basic tools & instruments delayed at the site due to holiday season, centralized back office instead of facilitating to make up for the delay, pushing site in-charge, and its team to give an innovative idea to implement in the plant. This type of misalignment can lead to a turbulent relationship difficult to manage at the site level.

Wherever possible data analytics to be employed for matching business priorities with Contractor supply chain capabilities as:

1. Understanding customer and supply chain uncertainties.

2. Evaluating the supply chain capacity

3. Achieving strategy fit.

Supply chain drivers are applicable for the service provider as:

o Facilities: Site facilities like office infrastructure, Site commuting vehicle, Guesthouse, etc.

o Inventory: Spare management and inventory management to maintain an optimum level

o Pricing: Discount pricing options can be used to utilize free resources. Likewise, more discount can be negotiated from sourcing partner by making a timely payment with the economy of scale

o Information: In current time real – time information can give an additional competitive advantage.

o Sourcing: Sourcing for placement agency, training and service experts, Auditors, etc.

All the drivers can be scaled on the spectrum for a complete range between efficiency and responsiveness.

Efficiency ⟶ Responsiveness

The Efficient system reduces the cost and responsiveness raise the customer satisfaction level. Customer preferences and willingness to pay premium form criteria to position on the above spectrum. Different customers with different priorities shall fall at a different position in spectrum and Service providers should be capable enough to use pricing (supply chain driver) to differentiate between premium and discount services as per customer requirement.

Better Collaboration

Information flow is a prominent challenge for companies. Integrated software solutions remove bottlenecks and allow for the seamless sharing of information, providing a big-picture view of the supply chain from end to end. Thanks to improved access to data, supply chain leaders have the information they need, in context, to make more informed decisions.

Improved Quality Control

process guidelines can help suppliers comply with your company's quality requirements. Some companies go beyond simply providing criteria, conducting periodic audits, or requesting documentation verifying suppliers' compliance steps. Implementing a Management Operating System (MOS) for monitoring key performance indicators includes:

- On-time delivery
- Scrap rates, rework and similar issues at suppliers
- Final product/service quality (as received by end customers)
- Time for complaint resolution
- Findings from supplier quality assessments

By analyzing performance data, companies can partner with the highest-performing vendors and suppliers to maintain strict quality control.

Higher Efficiency Rate

Having real-time data on the availability of required materials and delivery delays allows companies to implement backup plans, such as sourcing materials from a backup supplier, preventing further delays. Without real-time data, companies often don't have time to initiate plan B, resulting in issues such as out-of-stock inventory or late shipments to end consumers.

Keeping Up With Demand

This is one of the prominent challenges and has a large impact in a today's scenario with fluctuating service requirements. As customer plan may come up shutdown or contract revision with revision in resource deployment in a short period of time

Known as the bullwhip effect, this phenomenon often results from delays in communicating supply and demand changes. Supply chain leaders with access to real-time, accurate information and integrated data can better predict demand and readily respond to changing market conditions to avoid challenges like the bullwhip effect.

Shipping Optimization

Due to rising costs, shipping optimization is a priority for supply chain leaders. Identifying the most efficient shipping methods for small parcels, large bulk orders and other shipping scenarios helps companies get orders to customers faster while minimizing costs. Not only do those cost savings boost the company's bottom line, but savings can be passed on to consumers as well to improve customer satisfaction.

Maintenance/Service being a key function in any industry, timely delivery should be always on top priority.

Reduced Overhead Costs

Identifying unnecessary spending is another way to achieve leaner operations. If you're facing high logistics costs, for instance, switching to another provider offering the same service level and quality at a lower cost is a quick win.

Improved Risk Mitigation

Analyzing big-picture and granular supply chain data can reveal potential risks, enabling companies to put backup plans in place to readily respond to unexpected circumstances. By taking proactive action, rather than reacting to supply chain disruptions, quality control issues, or other concerns as they arise, companies can avoid negative impacts.

As in the case of the team mobilised at the site for commencement of contract on time but left out without required tools and materials becomes the cause of agony leading to customer un-satisfaction on a long term basis.

Improved Cash Flow

The benefits discussed above allow companies to make smarter decisions, choose the right partners, accurately predict and respond to market and demand changes and reduce supply chain disruptions, but that's not all: they also improve the company's bottom line. For example, working with reliable suppliers not only means fewer disruptions and more satisfied customers, but it also improves cash flow by allowing you to invoice (and get paid for products and services) sooner. Implementing more cost-effective solutions to eliminate wasteful spend and reducing overhead costs also contribute to positive cash flow.

Supply chain disruptions have a domino effect, impacting every juncture throughout the supply chain, but the same is true for the positives: effective supply chain management has direct and secondary effects that support the efficient, seamless flow of information, goods and services from procurement through final delivery.

Under the traditional form of Maintenance/Service procurement, the link between contracts and suppliers have typically concerned specific products and services priced to the lowest bidder. Thus multiple players have often functioned according to separate contracts with the client.

Now we move toward integrated supply chains wherein the members establish long-term relationships and group objectives. The benefits of a modern supply chain procurement process include:

- Higher overall profitability through lower real costs
- Reduced margins for equipment maintenance
- An increase in repeat pairing with progressive clients

- Better long-term project planning and coordination
- Better responsiveness from delivery facilities
- Fewer material defects
- Improved client satisfaction

AND the ability to establish great industry presence and reputation.

Implementing a time based Supply chain

Understanding the Supply Chain

Most firms view their supply chain as a single link and unidirectional. The single link is the link between the contractor and its direct supplier, which is typically the vendor. Unidirectional just means that the link is "one way." In other words, most firms look at their supply chain as only being about the flow of physical product from the various vendors to the maintenance outsourcing firm. This view is very limiting and will keep the maintenance outsourcing contractor firm from realizing the benefits of defining its supply chain more broadly.

In large outsourcing agencies the SCM of different sites are managed centrally from back office having benefit of optimization but system inertia can create delay in approvals & execution of supply.

The Maintenance outsourcing contracting firm's supply chain is neither single link nor unidirectional; rather, it is both multi-link and bidirectional. The supply chain includes all the links needed to span from the material, equipment to the crew in the field that will effectively maintain the material and equipment at the customer site. Some of these links, such as the manufacturer and distributor of Tools, PPE etc., are outside the electrical contracting firm's organization while others, such as crew deployed at site, are within the company's organization.

Similarly, the supply chain is bidirectional with two separate but interdependent channels. One channel involves the movement of physical product between the supplier and the field. The other channel involves the movement of information through the supply chain. Often, the information channel and its importance are not recognized. Instead, the focus is on the physical product flow with little emphasis on the information flow. In reality, procurement is really about effective and efficient information flow. The product flow is just a by-product or the result of the information flow.

Active Supply-Chain Management

Active supply-chain management is based on the belief that the purchasing function, interacting with its external suppliers and internal customers, has tremendous potential to add value. The goal of supply-chain management is to provide materials and equipment to the field at the highest delivered value for the lowest delivered cost. The supply-chain management mindset continually seeks to manage and leverage the skills of its supply chain in order to increase field productivity and reduce overall site operation cost.

In order to achieve its goals, the firm must actively manage its supply base. This means that the suppliers that compose its supply base must be carefully selected based on their ability to add value to the Maintenance outsourcing firm's business and integrated into a seamless supply chain.

In addition, there must be a continuous evaluation and feedback between the Maintenance outsourcing firm and its supply chain.

Factors in Selecting a Supplier

The five factors that need to be considered in the development and maintenance of a supply chain for material at site are addressed below.

- Required quality. Can the supplier provide the required quality on a consistent basis? Quality is typically set by the contract documents that include the technical specifications. However, required quality in this case may exceed that required by the specifications if improved material and equipment quality will reduce material handling costs, increase installation productivity and reduce rework. Increased material and equipment quality that results in increased material and equipment costs can result in a payback for the Maintenance outsourcing firm.

- Availability and delivery. Will the needed materials and equipment be available in the needed quantities and delivered on time? Stock outs and missed delivery schedules can be very expensive and disrupt the construction process. The cost of stock outs and missed delivery schedules can be totally out of proportion to the value of items purchased. Supplier capabilities and reputation for on-time delivery is a matter of prime importance when selecting a supplier.

- Efficient information flow. Efficient information flow that includes payment is another important consideration. How willing is the supplier to adjust its procedures to meet the electrical contracting firms and project's needs? Innovative ways of improving the efficiency of information flow, which includes the use of information technology, can pay tremendous dividends. Both the electrical contracting firm and the supplier can benefit a lot from being flexible and seeking ways to streamline information flow.

- Ongoing support. Can the supplier provide the necessary ongoing support needed to ensure customer satisfaction and peace of mind for the electrical contracting firm? Ongoing support is important in the traditional distribution market but it is critical in the voice/data/video (VDV) market, where constant technological change and the need to upgrade hardware and software is the norm. As customers become more quality conscious and demanding, ongoing support will become more important.

- Competitive price. Lastly, price is a factor. Can the supplier provide a competitive price? Notice that the question refers to "competitive price," not "lowest price." The objective here is to purchase materials and equipment based on lowest installed cost and not the lowest price. This requires that all the factors that affect the installation cost be considered, of which initial price is just one factor.

Managing the Supply Chain

The three aspects of supply-chain management, include supplier selection, supplier orientation and supplier evaluation.

Supplier selection: The selection of a supplier is critical and, as discussed previously, should involve more than just price. Selection of a supplier should be based on its ability to provide the right quality, in the right quantity, at the right place and at the right time. Only after all of these other factors have been considered should price be a consideration.

Supplier orientation: Once selected, the supplier should be oriented to the firm's procedures and business philosophy as well as the project's needs. The supplier must understand the electrical contracting firm's needs and expectations if it is to be an effective partner. Failure of the firm to communicate its needs and expectations to the supplier is a common problem in supplier relationships.

Supplier evaluation: Finally, there must be an ongoing supplier evaluation and feedback to ensure that the supplier is meeting the electrical contracting firm's needs and expectations. The most effective method of handling this is an internal survey of supplier performance followed by a compilation of responses, which forms the basis for an annual sit-down review with the supplier. In this sit-down review, continuous improvement of service and not price should be the focus.

Supply-Chain Management Benefits

Supply-chain management will provide benefits and new opportunities for the maintenance outsourcing contracting firm. Supply-chain management will result in an increased dialogue between the maintenance contracting firm and its suppliers and typically results in narrowing the maintenance contracting firm's supply base due to the development of long-term supplier agreements, partnerships and alliances. Changing the focus of the supplier relationship from price to service will lead to innovative transaction management, improved procurement planning and scheduling and better inventory management. In addition, taking advantage of supplier skills and expertise as a partner will lead to lower installed material and equipment costs through a variety of innovative procurement practices. These practices include custom fabrication, prefabrication and bundling. These practices should reduce both material handling and installation costs in the field.

Parts Pooling

Large OEM service provider operating multiple sites with similar or same assets can support their customer in reducing inventory of expensive parts and increase service levels by parts pooling and inter-warehouse or location exchange programs. A centralized inventory planning team of the organization can play a crucial role in the pooling process from identifying the pooling location, pooling stock, and pooling quantity to supporting the locations in day-to-day transfers of stock. Customer won't mind to pay some substantial fees to hold such essential inventory on his behalf.

VIEWPOINT

- In good reputed coaching institute with big hoardings in town displaying successful aspirants, we can see two groups of students which even BD – coaching business, classifies as rankers and bankers. Rankers with photograph and% score on hoarding are responsible for positioning in market and future business. Bankers are financing the business.

This is brilliant example of discounting performers at cost of financiers.

Chapter 6

Performance Monitoring of Maintenance Contract

"Confidence comes not from always being right but from not fearing to be wrong."

– Peter McIntyre

Introduction

As with most business operations, success really boils down to money that is spent as well as money that is saved and thus the ensuing profit margin. A contract that performs well does not allow trivial issues to derail progress or lead to unforeseen expenditures to get things back on track. Of course, in addition to the general economic impact that a bad contract can cause, relationships and reputations can be damaged. Thus, to determine whether contract performance is occurring as stipulated, it is important to look at the progress of the contract, as well as the overall impact that the contract has had on the company budget and its standing within the industry. Regular tracking and monitoring is a key characteristic of performance measurement. Contract monitoring is a process with appropriate tools of ensuring that a service provider adequately performs a service contract.

Maintenance Service Performance Measurement

Any organization outsource maintenance services to pursue a variety of objectives, including cost saving, realizing greater efficiency, managing risks, and improving service delivery. Furthermore, the benefit of contract cannot be realized if the performance of contractor is not assessed and monitored. Good contract monitoring system shall comprise of-

- Clearly identified KPI.
- Outlining performance-monitoring methodology.
- Defining frequency for KPI.
- Analysis and correction for KPI in case of external/Environmental factors.

Inadequate performance monitoring is not in line with good management practice and lead to deviate the operation from its objectives and may cause-

- Poorly established criteria for evaluating vendor performance.
- More focus on process with little or no emphasis on outcomes.
- Failure to conduct follow up reviews to evaluate the corrective action, if taken.
- Failure to identify the risk associated to Asset with different service providers.

Good management and supervision requires follow-up, feedback, and enough awareness of what is occurring to avoid unpleasant surprises.

Perquisites for Performance Based Contracts

Successful performance based contracts require;

- Sufficient dedicated fiscal resources and realistic performance parameter.
- Continuous training and capacity building to execute the contracts.
- Clear baseline data is needed to establish and monitor performance indicators and standards.
- Simple performance indicator and user monitoring can improve contract performance.

Address challenges like equipment overloading/improper operations and necessary modifications.

Key Performance Indicators (KPI)

The organization business objective forms the basis of broader KPI, to refine to micro level as per industry specific requirement.

- Timeliness
- Cost of service
- Quality and improvement of service
- Occupation Health and safety
- Customer satisfaction

Key Performance Indicators (KPI) is now very popular among industries and forms scale for measuring progress and achieve predefined goals against contracts. KPI to be designed with lot of thought and used optimally. Moreover, KPI needs to be realistic.

KPI are used to measure the effectiveness of the maintenance management solution that directly impacts assets/equipment performance and total maintenance cost.

KPI can be different in different industries ongoing trends, to be monitored periodically. KPI should in line with common objectives. Some of them can be as:

a. Enhanced equipment/Asset Life

b. Improves labor productivity.

c. Reduce downtime, improving productivity.

d. Minimizes inventory investments,

   And

e. Lower the total cost of maintenance.

These can be direct KPI or in many cases it is final aggregate evolved out by weightage of different component on the scale of say 100 giving single figure.

Now with advancement in analytics dynamic KPI can be depicted, using mathematical modeling to work out depending variable as function of all independent variables and that too in real time to incorporate any possible correction there itself, without waiting for monthly report.

Very simple example is if a person want to improve on driving skills for better fuel efficiency, He has to fill fuel in some fixed quantity and drive for certain Kms. Then calculate Kms/Ltr. Even all errors in fuel metering and Milometer and manual adds up. Then change the driving practice as reducing clutch operation etc. for next possible span and compare. Although it may give fair idea but too tidy process.

In present generation of car you directly get the value of Km/Ltr on display in real time. You can use this as output, adopting different driving styles as variables and come out with optimum one to be later developed as habit.

All KPI can be drawn on dashboard with varying color as Yellow, green and red. These color code let you see at a glance which areas are critical and needs your urgent attention, and which are currently under control.

Now a days, in such competitive environment with continuous cost pressure, customer insists for KPI assigned with Bonus/Penalty clause. More specifically, effective monitoring requires that contractors be incentivized to perform. Incentives are the mechanisms that motivate contractors and maintain accountability through threat of penalty.

Designing of KPI (In Line With Clear Goal and Objectives)

KPI to be framed clear and crisp, aligned with industrial goal and objective can be denoted as "SMART" KPI.SMART is an abbreviation stands for Specific, Measurable, Achievable, Relevant and Timely and to be used to guide for defining KPI. These KPI should accurately monitor the plant performance against time.

To make sure your objective are clear and reachable, each one should be:

- Specific: Every KPI should be well defined, clear and unambiguous.

- Measurable: As we all know, what cannot be measured also cannot be controlled. KPI specific criteria that measures progress toward accomplishment of the goal. Any deviation from desired path to be timely addressed to bring it in control.

- **A**chievable: Attainable and not impossible to achieve. i.e. KPI to be realistic and not to be misused as mean to impose penalty on contractor. As in some cases the contractor will built up penalty in contingency, inflating the cost of the contract.

- **R**elevant: Within reach, realistic and relevant to specific industry. It can be achieved within defined timeline and with available resources.

- **T**imely: With a clearly defined timeline, including a starting date and target date. All activities & events are assigned with time.

Examples of SMART Maintenance KPI

- Reduced Energy consumption 10% annually for 2 years.

- Improve System reliability, Reducing Unplanned downtime by 50% annually.

- Improving availability, With increasing span between Planned maintenance.

- Improving SFC / Plant heat rate & SLOC in Power plants. Here various correction factor as Calorific value of fuel, Ash content and other environmental conditions are to be incorporated in formula.

Maintenance Metrics

Maintenance KPIs and maintenance metrics are often used interchangeably. However, there's a difference between the two.

KPIs are numbers that tie organizational progress to maintenance performance, while metrics connect maintenance performance to maintenance actions. In other words, maintenance KPIs are a target your business is aiming at and maintenance metrics are the arrows you're shooting at that target.

Maintenance metrics are measurement that gives you insight into how different people and equipments are interlinked and operating at your facility. They quantify the daily activity of maintenance and their impact on asset performance.

Having the numbers makes it easier to detect strengths, weakness and opportunity for improvement. Metrics gives us a complete picture of everyday tasks, which give control over your maintenance operation and practical way to improve work.

For example, the ultimate goal of any maintenance organization might be to reduce inventory cost. But upfront it appears to be big challenge. This challenge can be addressed with multiple small action (can be taken as improvement idea, Kaizen etc.) like accurate assessment of failure rate, Inventory accuracy. These are maintenance matrices.

Common Maintenance Metrics

Everything in maintenance revolves around humans and machines. Optimising the performance of people and assets is crucial to maintenance success. There are three main categories of maintenance metrics – asset, operational and inventory metrics. Understanding each helps connect the dots between actions and impact, to take informed decisions towards facility up gradation.

Asset Performance Metrics

- Mean Time to repair
- Mean Time between failures
- Overall equipment effectiveness

Inventory Metrics

- Turnover Ratio
- Slow-moving parts percentage and
- Obsolete parts percentage

Mean Time to Repair (MTTR): MTTR is a maintenance metric that measures the average time required to troubleshoot and repair failed equipment. It indicates how quickly an organization can respond to unplanned breakdown and repair them.

MTTR calculates the period between the start of the incident and the moment the system returns to production. This takes into account the time to:

1. Notify technicians

2. Diagnose the issue.

3. Fix the issue

4. Allow the equipment to cool down

5. Reassemble, align and calibrate the asset.

6. Set up, test, and start up the asset for production.

This metric does not take into account lead-time for parts.

MTTR Calculation: The MTTR is calculated by dividing the total unplanned maintenance time spent on an asset by the total number of failures that asset experienced over a specific period. MTTR is usually represented in hours.

The MTTR calculation assumes that:

1. Tasks are performed sequentially

2. Tasks are performed by appropriately trained personnel.

MTTR = Total Maintenance time/Number of repairs

MTTR is dependent on several factors, like the type of assets, its criticality, approach, age etc.

Significance of MTTR: MTTR analysis can provide insight into the way your maintenance operations purchases equipment, Scheduled maintenance and completes tasks. Finally improvement in MTTR helps organization to remove inefficiencies in turn improving plant productivity.

MTTR can be used for making repair or replace decisions on aging assets. If an asset takes longer to repair as it ages, it may be more economical to replace it.

MTTR in business: Mean time to repair is a tool for evaluating the quality of a facility's maintenance practices and processes. It can also be used to investigate the value and performance of asset enabling organization to take smarter decision about asset management.

MTTR is a starting point for assessing efficiency and eliminating redundancies, roadblocks and confusion in maintenance to avoid needless downtime.

Mean Time between failures (MTBF): MTBF is the average time between system breakdowns. MTBF is a crucial maintenance metric to measure performance, safety and equipment design, especially for critical or complex assets, like generators or airplanes. This in broad term elaborate the reliability of an assets.

MTBF uses only unplanned maintenance and doesn't account for scheduled maintenance, like inspections, recalibrations, or preventive part replacement.

MTBF = No. of operational Hrs/No. of failures

Significance of MTBF: MTBF is use to anticipate how likely an asset is to fail within a certain time period or how often a certain type of failure may occur.

Overall equipment effectiveness (OEE): Overall equipment effectiveness is a maintenance KPI that measures an asset's level of productivity. OEE is a combination of three factors that tell you how efficient an asset is during the manufacturing process: Asset availability, Asset Performance, and

Production quality as

Availability: How often does the asset en function when needed?

Performance: How much does the asset produce?

Quality: How many high-quality items does the asset produce ?

When an asset operates with an OEE of 100%, it means that every item it produces is without defect (quality), it is producing as fast as possible (performance), and it experiences no unplanned downtime (availability).

OEE = Availability x Performance x Quality

Where **Availability** = Total Run Time of asset in Period/Total planned production time of an asset = (Total Run Time of asset + Stand by time of an asset) in period/Total time in period.

Availability states that equipment is available for rated production.

Performance of an asset = Actual system throughput/Maximum possible throughput

Quality = No. of units produced complying to quality standard/Total Units or Qty produced

Significance of OEE: Overall equipment effectiveness indicates of how efficient the manufacturing process is. It can be used to identify underperforming assets and correlates poor performance with one or more of the three main factors. Once the source of problem is identified it is fixed.

Overall equipment effectiveness is a tool for evaluating the efficiency of assets during the manufacturing process. It can also be used to investigate the people, processes and tools that impact how assets operate. When combined with the insight from other maintenance metrics, OEE provides a great foundation for identifying areas of an operation that can be improved and quantifiable way to measure progress.

Operational Metrics

- Planned Maintenance Percentage
- Preventive Maintenance Compliance

Planned Maintenance Percentage: PMP is a maintenance metric that measures the number of planned maintenance tasks in comparison to all maintenance tasks executed in a given period. This is expressed in percentage. PMP can be used to fix the cause of failure, inefficiencies and disrupted maintenances process.

PMP = Planned Maintenance Hrs./Total Maintenance Hrs X 100

Monitoring, analyzing and improving planned maintenance percentage can have a huge domino effect on the entire facility. Moving away from reactive maintenance to a proactive approach provides operation more control over its tasks, resource and money. PMP enhanced value indicates improved maintenance system and addressing weakness if any it helps in:

- Effective planning and scheduling of maintenances.
- Reduce downtime.
- Compliance to standards
- Cost in control

Preventive Maintenance Compliance (PMC): PMC is a measure of percentage PM tasks carried out on schedule in a specified time period.

PMC= No. of completed PM/No. of schedule PM X 100

PM compliance is most effective when used to improve a facility's preventive maintenance program with the goal of reducing downtime., PMC provide the mean to determine if a PM program is working well or not.

Measuring and improving PMC helps to increase accountability. Calculating PM compliance can also tell you if relevant PMs aren't being completed consistently. Once you can identify which important tasks are being skipped, you can begin to find out why. Reasons can include everything from a breakdown somewhere in the work order process to a lack of spare parts or a shortage of labour. Knowing where your resources and processes are lacking can help you find a solution and get your PMs back on schedule so critical assets get the attention they deserve.

PM compliance is also an important tool when preparing for audits. Auditors often look at a facility's PM program its level of compliance. Failing to comply with critical PMs can be a serious setback for organization and may attract penalty.

Inventory Metrics

- Turnover Ratio
- Slow-moving parts percentage and Obsolete parts percentage

KPI Indicators: Leading and lagging indicators are two types of measurements used when assessing performance in a business or organisation. A leading indicator is a predictive measurement, for example; the safety compliance is a leading indicator. A lagging indicator is an output measurement, for example; Limiting energy consumption to predetermined value can be lagging indicator. The difference between the two is a leading indicator can influence change and a lagging indicator can only record what has happened.

As we very well know Maintenance Metrics are used to measure and quantify the level of achievement of a particular asset or plant process. Determining the state of the plant using metrics and performance indicators enable personnel to make data-driven decisions and identify potential problems. Metrics and indicators are generally classified according to whether they predict future performance or describe past performance – these are referred to as leading or lagging indicators, respectively.

Leading Indicators

Leading indicators are measurements that predict the outcome of a process or an event. These indicators are measured and are considered to be precursors of events or situations.

An example of a leading indicator is schedule compliance, when regarded as an indicator of the likelihood that an asset will experience unplanned failures and downtime. Because schedule compliance describes the amount of planned maintenance activities done on time, it can be correlated with how effectively maintenance activities are carried out, and therefore relate to increasing reliability.

Similarly, the metric planned maintenance percentage can be considered as a leading indicator as it affects the amount of unplanned downtime by aiming to keep assets running at optimal health. It also affects the required manpower as planned maintenance activities can be more efficiently scheduled.

Lagging Indicators

Lagging indicators measure the performance of the plant by looking at the outcomes and results of processes and operations. By analyzing the historical trend of the performance of the plant and its parts, reactive strategies can be applied to address underlying issues.

Examples of lagging indicators include mean time to repair (MTR), mean time between failure (MTBF), and overall equipment effectiveness (OEE). Notice how these metrics are measured to confirm trends that have developed over time. Because these metrics are basically a historical record of performance, they can provide insights on which events in the past might have caused fluctuations to the plant's performance.

Using Leading and Lagging Indicators

From the previous discussion, you can imagine how one indicator that predicts the future and another that looks back at the past, can form a complete view of the performance of the plant over time. Leading and lagging indicators, together, aim to provide a panoramic view of the state of the plant through time.

The plant's maintenance manager is expected to identify a manageable set of key performance indicators (KPIs) – a mix of leading and lagging indicators viewed as a whole picture – to assess the plant's maintenance effectiveness.

VIEWPOINT

- Understanding the difference in expectations, when we do job ourselves vs outsourced to external agencies.

E.g. Small activities like cleaning personal vehicle, when we do ourselves expectations are relaxed, i.e we may reduce the frequency or skipfor days or even weeks in case of any other urgent job. But Once it is outsourced to someone for even Rs. 500, expectations are High with no compromise on quality or frequency.

Chapter 7

OHS in Maintenance Service

"You've got to get your team to not only understand your
company brand, but also understand their personal brand."

– Amber Hurdle

Introduction

As History shows us, a successful safety program starts with recognizing the
status quo isn't going far enough to protect workers. It involves documenting
the problem, working with regulators to set appropriate standards, and
educating your employees so they understand how to keep themselves safe.

Traditionally, maintenance tasks in companies were carried out
by specialised internal maintenance personnel. However, during the
last decades, there have been significant changes in the organisation of
maintenance activities. Nowadays, maintenance tasks might be shared by
operators and maintenance personnel, or partially or totally outsourced.
Maintenance has emerged as a commonly subcontracted function in the
industry.

These developments in the maintenance organisation have consequences
on health and safety. (Sub) contracting maintenance services is often
considered as an aggravating factor in terms of safety and health. A broad
analysis of a work accident database shows that maintenance workers were
the second most frequent victims of accidents related to subcontracting,
following closely after construction workers.

Outsourcing of maintenance activities may affect external workers' health and safety:

- if the work environment is unfamiliar;
- if the operations are fragmented (for instance maintenance workers do not know what has been performed prior to their own operations);
- if external personnel is improperly received:
- if there is no adequate monitoring/supervision of contractors' operations;
- if there is no internal contact person with specialist knowledge.

Industrial Customer leadership and commitment to the continuous improvement of health and safety is recognized as an important driver for improving health and safety performance throughout the supply chain. Therefore, when outsourcing maintenance, companies need to consider the health and safety implications of the job they want to be done and select a contractor who can demonstrate the necessary competencies for the work and who is also operating in accordance with appropriate health and safety systems. This requires integrating health and safety aspects into the procurement procedure and giving significant weighting to health and safety considerations in the selection and award criteria for the contract.

Guidance from the HSE suggests that to determine a contractor's competence companies may ask for information on:

- the experience they have in the type of work to be done;
- their health and safety policies and practices;
- their recent health and safety performance (number of accidents etc.);
- the qualifications and skills they have;
- their selection procedure for sub-contractors;
- the health and safety training and supervision they provide;
- their arrangements for consulting their workforce;

- if they have any independent assessment of their competence;

- if they are members of a relevant trade or professional body;

- whether they or their employees hold a 'certification' in health and safety training (e.g. safety card, etc.) from safety council or any recognized body. This is a growing trend in some industries.

The client needs to ensure that the contractor has an effective procedure for monitoring and auditing the competence of subcontractors. He must also ensure there are systems in place for providing information, instruction and training to the sub-contractor, When selecting a suitable sub-contractor, a contractor may use some or all of the criteria that a client uses in selecting a suitable contractor.

Statutory Compliance

Occupational safety and health directives transposed into the national legislation of the Member States set minimum standards of protection for workers and they also apply when companies use maintenance service providers. The Member States may have additional national requirements. Thus, it is important to take into consideration the legislation applicable in the relevant State(s).

The Framework Directive lays down the obligation of the employers to cooperate in implementing the safety and health provisions and coordinate their actions in matters of the protection of workers and prevention of occupational risks, where several undertakings share a workplace. and shall inform one another and their respective workers and/or workers' representatives of these risks.

This also stipulates that the employer ensures that contractors and their workers engaged in work in his undertaking and/or establishment receive adequate information and appropriate instructions concerning the safety and health risks and protective and preventive measures during their activities in his premises.

Buying Compliance – A Guideline for Social Considerations in Public Procurement Contract

The guide drafted by the Commission to explain the opportunities offered by the existing legal framework for public authorities to take into account social considerations in their public procurement, thus paying attention not only to price but also to the best value for money. The Guide has been produced primarily for public authorities, but in the hope that it will inspire private-sector purchasers too. The Guide follows the procurement procedure step by step, explaining how social considerations, for example, health and safety at work, can be taken into account at different stages of the procurement procedure.

For example, social considerations regarding labor conditions are generally more appropriate to be included in the contract performance clauses, as in general, they do not qualify as technical specifications or selection criteria, within the meaning of the Procurement Directives.

However, it is permitted into the technical specifications, for example, in a contract for works, the requirement for measures to avoid accidents at work, and specific conditions for the storage of dangerous products in order to safeguard the health and safety of workers.

When selecting suppliers, service providers, and contractors, tenderers can also be excluded for failure to comply with national legislation regarding health and safety at work.

Contracting authorities may also include in the contract performance clauses social considerations for subcontractors regarding, for example, health and safety requirements, Exceptionally, social considerations can be included in the award criteria for the contract as an 'additional criterion' to make the difference between two equal tenders.

Maintenance Related Standards

Standards are formal documents for the unification of material and non-material subjects (technical criteria, methods, processes, or practices). Standards ensure specific characteristics of services/products such as management, safety, environmental, and/or quality aspects. They present the state of the art processes or practices. Due to new safety requirements, new methods and materials, and technological evolution most standards require periodic revision.

Maintenance standards can contribute to the improvement of the service quality and the ability to demonstrate this to clients. Standards also provide benefits in terms of enhancing understanding and communication through common terminology and improved contractual relationship. They also help service providers to meet legislative and regulatory requirements related to health and safety.

Health and Safety Aspects in Maintenance Procurement

The procurement process including different steps can be elaborated as Owner Task, Service Provider/Contractor Task & Common Task)

Owner Responsibility

A. Definition of demands (range of services) and requirements

Simultaneously to the definition of the works and range of tasks, procedures should be established to ensure that national laws and regulations and the workplace's own health and safety and health requirements are identified and incorporated into the procurement procedure of maintenance services. The procurement strategy should include tender evaluation strategies and models that test the capability of bidders to meet health and safety specifications. Preparations for contractor selection should include setting criteria for the evaluation of their health and safety standards.

B. Selection of the contractor/service provider

An overview of general and health and safety related criteria for the selection of (sub) contractors, as well as indicators and sources of information, shall be as in Table below.

Table: Aspects/criteria, indicators and sources of information for the selection of (sub) contractors

Aspects/criteria	Indicators	Sources
Technical capability to perform the contract	• core activities of the company • experience in similar work • technical equipment • quality control system • skills and qualifications • special qualifications (e.g. welding according to ISO 9606)	• website of the company • portfolio of the bidder/tenderer • certificates • documentation on quality control system • references from other clients • Actual activity wise case study for addressing major issue.
Health and safety management	• health and safety policies • safe systems of work • health and safety training • health and safety performance • technical equipment and personal protective equipment	• general safety rules • safe work method statements • certifications for safety management (e.g. Safety Checklist Contractors) • quality management (e.g. ISO 9000) • health and safety management (e.g. OHSAS 18001) • environmental management (e.g. ISO 14001) • audits, accreditations • accidents and health statistics of the service provider

Aspects/criteria	Indicators	Sources
Selection and supervision of subcontractors	• procurement management of the tenderer • supervision system	• documentation on the selection of sub-contractors • audits • other communication
Abnormally low tenders/tenders with the risk of low health and safety standards	• calculations of costs • time schedules	• content of the tender/bid • workshops • communication with bidder/tenderer

The public procurement directives permit contracting authorities in States that have provided for this possibility in their national legislation to exclude from a public procurement procedure any candidate or tenderer who has not respected the provisions of such legislation. These exclusion clauses can include, for example, non-compliance with provisions on health and safety.

Site-Specific Safety Rules and Working Conditions

After the selection of a bidder/tenderer, the client provides information on the site-specific safety rules and working conditions.

Contractor/Service Provider Action Plan

1. Assessment of competences and resources, preparation of the bid/tender

When an open request for quotation/tender is published, the (possible) bidder/tenderer (maintenance service provider) checks the demands and requirements) and considers them against its own capabilities and resources.

Numerous companies publish codes of conduct listing general rules of supplier behavior. Corporate social responsibilities (CSR) reports also provide information on companies' guiding principles in the social and environmental areas, which they apply in their business operations and in their interactions with stakeholders. Additionally, there are different information platforms for business and procurement, which provide information on procurement and safety measures.

2. Presentation of the bid/tender

If there is a need for comprehensive, long-term cooperation between client and service provider(s) (e.g. in process industries), presenting the bid/tender during a moderated workshop can be helpful, and even essential in some cases. Safety concepts and standards should be discussed in detail during the presentation.

Common Tasks (Owner & Service Provider/Contractor)

1. On-site inspection

On-site inspections help to minimize misunderstandings between the client and the contractor. Safety rules should be discussed and cleared at the worksite before the actual work starts. Potential additional risks on the site have to be regarded and additional measures should be agreed on if necessary.

2. Agreement on responsibilities, duties and contact persons

The agreement on roles and responsibilities and duties is another essential step in procurement. It includes appointing a coordinator, nominating supervisors and contact persons, and defining communication structures.

3. Coordination of tasks and time management

If maintenance is not carried out during plant shutdowns good coordination between production and maintenance staff is needed. When there are multiple contractors and multiple activities on-site at the same time, a solid project plan and work schedule are needed in order to prevent interference. Within the planning process, time-critical risks and buffer time should be considered, too. While the primary concern is health and safety, adequate coordination of the contractors' work and how they fit into an overall project plan or on-going process as well as thorough communication will also increase efficiency.

4. Risk assessment

The risk assessment for maintenance activities requires particularly good cooperation between the contractor and the client: the participation of both parties is necessary for adequate risk assessment(s).

The risk assessment should be carried out and signed off by the client and the contractor before maintenance starts. Further details about this are summarized as 'Safe maintenance – working with contractors and subcontractors'.

5. Preparation and signing of the contract

Once the previous steps have been completed the service contract can be drawn up. In addition to clauses on technical, financial, and legal issues, it is good practice for requirements related health and safety to be included in the contract. This is a good way of making the contractor aware of the client's requirements for health and safety, and where their responsibilities.

The signing of the contract is a formal act and once it has been done the service provider(s) can start work. The safety and health aspects of working with maintenance contractors are the subject of the specific documents 'Safe maintenance – working with contractors and subcontractors'.

6. Post-contract assessment

The contract and its annexes will contain detailed information on the services to be carried out. However, changes might occur while the work is taking place. A post-contract assessment should be done to enable future improvements to be made on issues like the maintenance strategy, the work process, and the interaction between the client and the contractor. Ideally, both parties should collect data, and record experiences and knowledge throughout the entire maintenance process. This input can be used as feedback for the client and/or contractor in order to improve their technical, organizational, and health and safety performance as well as for future reference.

Conclusion (Decision Taking)

Feature	Negative	Marginal	Neutral	Effective	Remarks
Long term Effectiveness		√			
Potential of scope enhancement		√			
Benchmark/KPI up gradation		√			
Incentive to outsource				√	Work load flexibility & Expertise
Direct cost effectiveness	√				Selective point specific positive.
Systems/Operation Effects			√		
Organizational Effectiveness effect		√			
Human resources and culture		√			
Vendor related effects			√		
Contract agreement					Yes
Recommendation	Avoid	Re – evaluate & Review		GO	

Some basic safety terminology in context: This is just indicative and to be aligned with industry/Site documented process.

S.no	Concept	Brief Description
1	Hierarchy of controls	a. Eliminate b. Substitute c. Engineering control d. Administration Controls e. PPE
2.	Zone classification in hazardous area	method of analyzing and classifying the environment where explosive gas atmospheres may occur so as to facilitate the proper selection and installation of equipment to be used safely in that environment. Hazardous areas are classified into 3 zones based upon the frequency of the occurrence and duration of an explosive gas atmosphere, as follows: Zone 0 – Area in which an explosive gas atmosphere is present continuously or for long periods or frequently. Zone 1 – Area in which an explosive gas atmosphere is in which an explosive gas atmosphere is likely to occur in normal likely to occur in normal operation operation occasionally occasionally. Zone 2 – Area in which an explosive gas atmosphere is not likely to occur in normal operation but, if it does occur, will persist will persist for a short period for a short period only. Non hazardous area (safe area) – A non hazardous area is an area in which an explosive atmosphere is not expected to be present.

Continued...

3.	Tool box talk	A tool box talk is an informal safety meeting that focuses on safety topics related to the specific job, such as workplace hazards and safe work practices. Tool box talks meetings are sometimes referred to as tailgate meetings of safety briefings.
4.	Work permit	Permit-to-work System is a formal written system used to control certain types of work which are potentially hazardous. It is also a mean of communication among site personnel to ensure all necessary safety precautions are taken before commencing such work.
		Refer site specific work permit system in case of contract management responsibility shall be clearly defined and assigned to owner and contractor.
5.	Positive Energy Isolation Process includes listing location with number of devices. Identification of Circuit in operation with special means to be provided to hold parts, save information, local lighting etc. ensuring operator safety, LOTO process… etc. should be well documented and followed religiously.	Isolation and Energy dissipation A procedure which consists of all the four following actions: Isolating [disconnecting, separating] the machine (or defined parts of the machine) from all power supplies; Locking (or otherwise securing) all the isolating unit in the isolating position; Dissipating or restraining any stored energy which may give rise to a hazard. NOTE Energy may be stored in e.g.: Mechanical parts continuing to move through inertia; Mechanical parts liable to move by gravity; Capacitances, Pressurized fluids; Springs. Verifying by a mean of a safe working procedure that the actions taken according to a), b) and c) above have produced the desired results.

Occupational Health & Safety Management System

Whenever, production plants like Aluminium refinery, steel plants, oil and gas production plants, automobile manufacturing plant equipment manufacturing like cars, air conditioner are to be designed and operated; associated hazards and risks also follows.

The Entropy Model

There are two categories of risks that are present in all the systems.

1. Inherent or residual risk – This comes from the design stage and cannot be completely eliminated. E.g. Aeroplane tires, Underpass, and overpass not provided for railway crossings.

2. Entropy Risk – This is caused by the degradation of the company systems. (Entropy is a measure of degradation or disorganization of the universe) Eg. Boiler explosion, Brakes failure, Power failures.

System degradation factors:

i. Processes – Work practices

ii. Technology – Plant, Equipment, tools, and chemicals

iii. The physical environment – Locational and structural factors

iv. Human resources – People

Residual or Entropic Risk = p x t x p e x h

Where p – process risk score, t – technology risk score, p e – physical environment risk score and h – human resources risk score

When there is any loss of integrity deterioration keeps happening. Deterioration occurs due to maintenance or operation problem and system reaches to ALARP level

As residual risks are inherent in the design stage, it is designer responsibility to look into all aspects as Process, technology, physical environment, Human resources to limit risk to ALARP (**As low as reasonably practical**)

Service provider/contractor has very little control over it and initially contractor curb to limit Entropy risk by carrying out proper and timely maintenance, the later Service provider can review the residual hazard during operation and minimize by necessary modification and improvement recommendations.

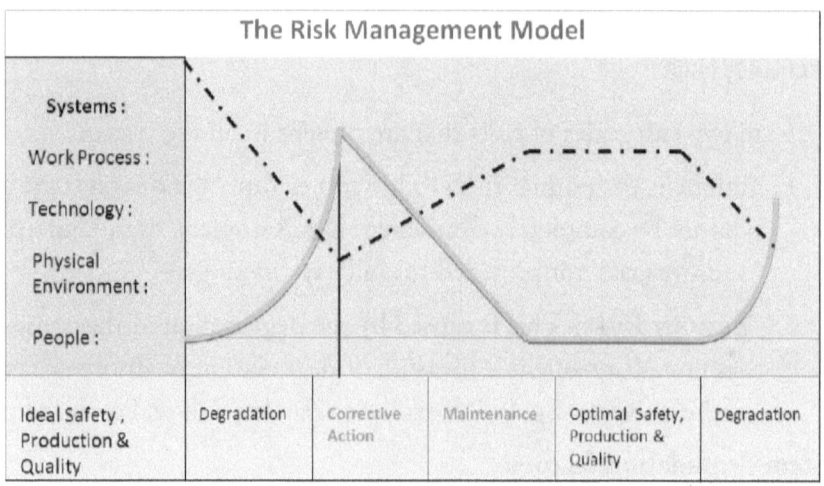

Safety Performance Indicators

Hazard Initiating Mechanisms (IM's) are responsible for the incidents and associated consequences. Safety Performance Indicator (SPI) provides measures to evaluate the performance of risk Control Systems put into use to control these IM's. We have to find out these SPI, apply analytics for prevention and prescription. Measurement of these indicators leads to confidence as:

- Too many organizations rely on failure data to monitor performance indicating risks are adequately controlled. i.e. Loss time incidence (LTI), fatalities, minor injuries, etc.

- For major hazard installations, process safety risks will be a significant aspect of business risk, asset integrity, and reputation.

- Discovering weakness in control systems by having a major incident is too late and too costly for correction.

- Early warning through measurement of dangerous deterioration within a critical system provides an opportunity to avoid major incidents.

Active Monitoring and Reactive Monitoring

Process safety indicators can provide an early warning, before catastrophic failure, that critical controls have deteriorated to an acceptable level.

Active Monitoring provides feedback on performance before an accident or an incident.

Reactive monitoring involves identifying and reporting on incidents to check the controls in place or adequate, to identify weaknesses or gaps in control systems, and to learn from mistakes.

Leading Indicators:

Leading indicators are a form of active monitoring focused on a few critical risk control systems to ensure their continued effectiveness.

Leading indicators require a routine systematic check that key activities or actions are undertaken or intended. So leading indicators talks about the Effectiveness of the system. E.g. Compliance with inspection schedules.

Lagging Indicators:

Lagging indicators are a form of reactive monitoring requiring the reporting of specific incidents and events to discover the weakness of the system. These incidents or events do not have to result in major damage or injury or even a loss of containment, providing that they represent a failure of a significant control system that fails or guards against or limits the consequences of a major incident.

Lagging indicators show when a desired safety outcome has failed or not has been achieved. Lagging Indicators describes System Weakness. Eg. Rusted scaffolding, Loose bolts.

Leading and lagging indicators are set in a structured and systematic way for each critical task control system within the whole process of safety management. In tandem, they work as system guardians providing dual assurance to confirm that the risk control system is operating as intended or providing a warning that problems are starting to develop. Leading and lagging indicators both are equally useful for the OH&S Management system.

Tolerance should be defined for each leading indicator. This represents the point at which deviation in performance should be flagged up for the attention of senior management. E.g. ' percentage of overdue safety-critical maintenance actions'.

Accident investigation

Accident/incident investigations focus on identifying the root cause instead of finding fault/blame. The accident investigation is carried out in two phases.

Phase I: Incident logging

This includes logging of basic incident detail either by victim or worker and supervisor present at the time of the incident. Information includes the location of the incident, the activity involved, immediate cause notice, incident narrative, risk score, etc.

Phase II: Incident Investigation

In cases where risk score is high, further investigations take place by a team of supervisors. Recommendations are made on the basis of findings from the investigation.

Incident Investigation process and flow diagram, however, varies from industry to industry but the basic objective remains to identify the root cause and address the associated issue to ensure accidents does not happen

Information Structure in the incident report (IR): Information should cover all aspects of the incident and broad framework shall necessarily comprise of

Processes

- Were the safety procedure Inadequate ?
- Were the safety procedure not available?

- Was the safety procedure not followed ?
- Was the procedure followed incorrectly or there is further scope of improvement in process ?

Technology

- Was the technology in safe operational condition?
- Was the correct technology used for the task?
- Were there any other factors related to the condition, operation, maintenance, which may have contributed to the incident?

Physical Environment

- Did any environmental factors contribute to the accident?
- Was there free, safe access to the location?

Human Resources

- Was the person concerned was doing his/her normal duties?
- Was the person using appropriate PPE in proper manner ?
- How was the person normal behavior while doing work, and was he competent to do the assigned job?
- Was the person trained on its safety procedure?

Assessment of Severity: Risk Score Calculation

Probability

1. High probability of occurring
2. Moderate probability of occurring
3. Low probability of occurring
4. Very low probability of occurring
5. Rarely occurring

Consequences

	A	B	C	D	E
1	1	2	4	7	11
2	3	5	8	12	16
3	6	9	13	17	20
4	10	14	18	21	23
5	15	19	22	24	25

Consequences (on Human/Property):

A. Fatality/System loss/Property damage of huge monetary loss.

B. Severe injury/major property damage/major system loss

C. Minor injury/Minor system loss/Minor property damage.

D. Medical treatment case/Property damages with small monetary loss.

E. Minor Property damage/First Aid

Guidelines for Investigation

The investigation should commence immediately for high risk incidents. Investigation Techniques to be well defined and clear to the team.

Following steps should be followed to carry out investigation:

- Visit the site (for high risk incident)
- Collect and analyse the evidences (Physical and human)
- Listing the findings from analysis
- Preparing report with corrective action.

Investigation techniques followed should be able to identify basic facts from evidences:

- What has happened?
- What was the effect and who/what was effected?
- What happened just before and after the incident i.e. chain of events.
- What was the operational and environmental conditions during incident ? (use photograph, sketches, interview of the personnel involved)?

Formation of Investigation Team

- Team should be cross functional as far as possible.
- Team should comprise of following personnel

- o Area/Site Expert
- o Investigation techniques expert
- o Site/Area safety professional
- o HR/IR personnel
- For high risk score, team should be led by senior management, such as safety chief
- For medium risk score, team should be led by section head.
- For low risk score, team leader should be site/section manager.

Once Investigation over with immediate and intermediate cause analysis, next step to process to Root cause analysis.

Root Cause Analysis

During root cause analysis, identify key factors associated to four system components.Key factors are those circumstances that may have contributed to the incident's occurrence even though a clear logical connection cannot be found.Some common analysis technique are:

- Why why Analysis
- Fish bone Analyis
- Human factor Analysis
- Barrier analysis

All collected Investigation data's are evaluated with proper sequencing of logics to conclude the root cause of incident and is followed by submission of report and recommendations.

Recommendation and release of report

Past recommendation should be searched to find if it is a repeat of similar incidents.Recommendations should be smart:

- Specific & Precise
- Measurable
- Acheivable

- Relevant
- Time bound

After making the recommendations, the team should submit the report to the site/Area Head.

The report must comprise of:

- Information on effected particulars
- Facts of incident
- Detail of evidences.
- Technical analysis of evidences
- Finding from Analysis
- Recommendation for corrective actions.

The head should examine the report on the basis of

- Effectiveness of the recommendation
- Quality of data collected.
- Investigation techniques adopted.
- Reference to past incidents and recommendations

Safety Analytics

The data comprising of different attribute collected in structure format. Different information is retrieved from past record for analysis with an objective to provide descriptive analysis of the data.

Some of the attributes can be enlisted as below;

1. Month/Date
2. Location
3. Incident/Event
4. Working condition
5. Machine condition
6. Observation type

7. Incident type

8. Employee type

9. Time shift

For Example data can be tabulated for past three year (Say around 700 datas) these data can be represented under different category monthly basis, weekly basis or location/Department basis. The point of high frequency can be correlated with events and provide subject for indepth analysis. i.e. frequency percent is high on Sunday particular department indicates and provide the criteria to proceed for detail analysis and address the issue to bring in control.

May be Sunday being holiday causing lack of supervision or non availability of some special tool due to closure of workshop can be reason of high percentage of accidents on Sunday.

	N	Range	Minimum	Maximum	Sum	Mean		Std. Deviation	Variance
	Statistics	Statistics	Statistics	Statistics	Statistics	Statistics	Std. Errors	Statistics	Statistics
Working Temperature	700	15	30	45	18818	37.64	.193	4.306	18.541
Health Rating	700	9	1	10	2809	5.62	.117	2.607	6.798
Valid N (Listwise)	700								

Time series data can be represented in a different format as a Scatter plot, Histogram, etc.

Analytics can be used in pictorial form to represent different parameters as a comparison of incidents with contract employees and self employees. Contract employees are more prone to accidents as many contractors are coming from diverse backgrounds. Contract employee may be continuously changing and unfamiliar with sites may lead to more incidents. One more reason can be contractors are direct contact with machines and employees are more into white-collar jobs with activity including planning and supervision only.

No. of Incident vs time shift (for employees and contractor) can be plotted on scatter plot with the maximum fit line passing through the point.

Similarly, the histogram can be drawn to represent the incident occurring in different shifts and indicates an increase in the Evening shift.

Pattern in Time Series Data

- Average: the mean of observations over time. i.e. incidents over week, month etc.

- Trend: A gradual increase or decrease in the average over time. i.e Trend varies through the period right from project stage to maintenance and throughout lifecycle.

- Seasonal influence: Predictable short term cyclic behavior. Some trends which repeats on seasonal basis as some issue of incidents due to leakage current and equipment exposed to rain etc.

- Cyclical movement: unpredictable long – term cycling behavior due to business cycle or product/service life cycle.

- Random Error: remaining variation that cannot be explained by the other four components.

Control chart analysis

Control chart analysis also exhibit different types of patterns. Control chart ultimately identify the assignable cause with specific reasons for the behavior of the system in terms of accident occurrences.

Control charts

- Control chart is a technique widely used in on line quality monitoring of product.

- It is a tool which determines whether a process/system with characterstics of interest is in control or not.

- In safety, we use control chart to analyze the performance of system with respect to incidents reported.

- The procedures for control chart involve

    i. Computation of upper limit (UCL), Central line (CL) and Lower control limit (LCL),

ii. Plot of observations against the control limits.

- If the observations are within UCL and LCL, hen the system is in control, otherwise out-of control.

- Two important variables which are analyzed are:

  - Time between Occurrence (TBO) of incident.

  - Number of Incidents (NOI) per month.

A typical control chart

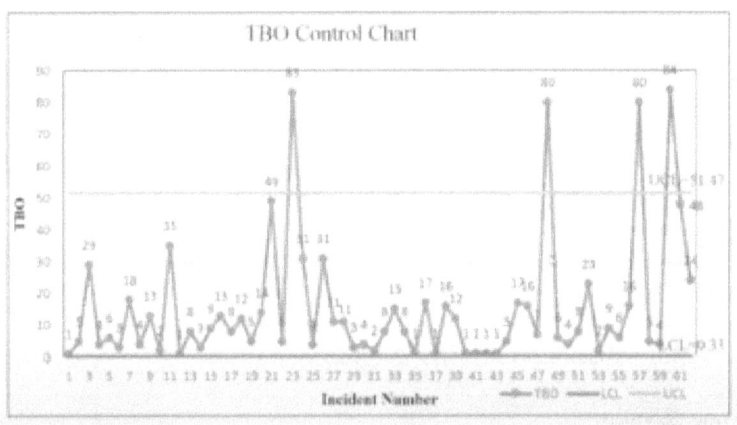

Number of incidents per Month (NOI)	Time between occurrence (TBO)
• NOI is a discrete variable	• TBO is a continuous variable
• NOI follows poisson distribution	• TBO follows weibull or exponential distribution
• NOI lower is the better and desirable	• TBO is greater the better variable
• As NOI is ' lower the better' type variable, the UCL value for NOI is representative of worst possible situation in the system under the existing condition.	• Its UCL can be thought of a TBO value that is achievable for the system considered.
	• LCL value for TBO shows the worst possible value of TBO under existing condition of operation.

Analysis of safety variable using control chart

Regression Model

Regression is general technique for data analysis, not limited to accident data. Regression mode is very useful in Predictive analysis. There are different statistics softwares like minitab, python, R etc. to execute regression model with large amount of data.

Predictive Analysis

- Predictive analysis is the practice of extracting insight from the existing data set with the help of data mining, statistical modeling and machine learning technique and using it to predict unobserved/unknown events.

- Identifying the cause-effect relationship across the variable for historical data.

- Discovering hidden insight and pattern with the help of data mining technique.

- Apply observed patterns to unknown in the past, present or future.

Prediction-Method

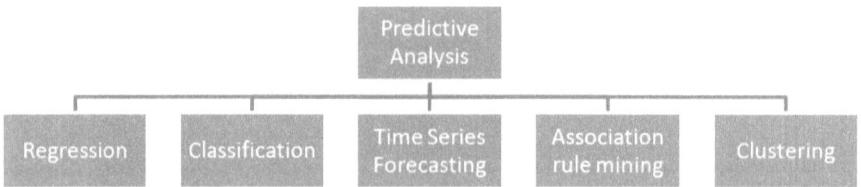

In any situation there shall be dependent variable and set of independent variables. Dependent variable are the variable whose values and occurrence are dependent on independent variables.

Incident rate = f (safety initiatives) – Incident rate is function of safety initiative.

$Y = \beta_0 + \beta_1 X_1 + \beta_2 X_2 + \beta_3 X_3 + \epsilon$ – Regression model stating relationship between incident rate (Y) and independent variable, which are safety initiatives.

In case of Y is any safety parameters say, Number of Incident in month (NOIM). Regression model for same can be worked out as ;

$$NOIM = \beta_0 + \beta_1 * Insp + \beta_2 * Trg + \beta_3 UA + e$$

Where, Insp – Inspection, Trg – training, UA – Unsafe Act are considered to be independent variable. The objective here is to find all parameter, driving error e to minimum.

Data Matrix

Data (Tentative) is tabulated in format in following structure for say past 30 months

S.No.	NOIM	Insp	Trg	UA	S.No.	NOIM	Insp	Trg	UA
1	3	15	10	12	-	-	-	-	-
2	4	23	12	9	-	-	-	-	-
3	4	22	13	10	28	2	24	6	4
-	-	-	-	-	29	5	13	6	3
-	-	-	-	-	30	3	22	6	4

Scatter Plot

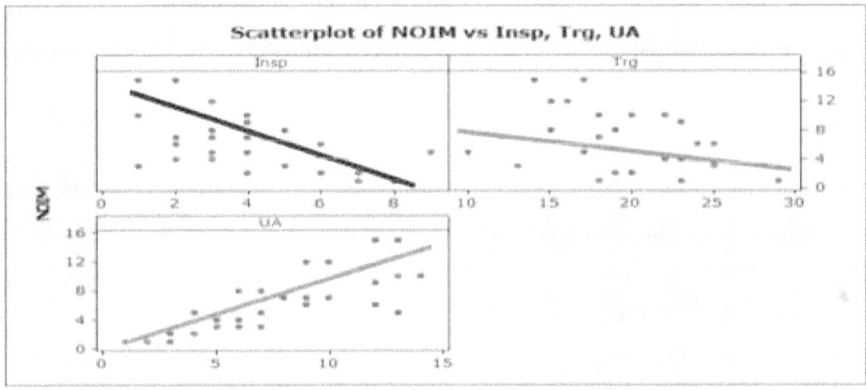

Regression model can be plotted with all past data and plot on scatter diagram and make out a close fit with minimum outliers. The linear relationship between independent and dependent variable can be plotted.

The values taken are hypothetical for reference only, but plotted curve meets the required characteristic as UA represent direct proportionality and Inspection & training indicates inverse relation with training and inspection i.e. increasing training and inspection leads to reduction in NOIM (Number of accident in month)

Using mathematical model and running through appropriate analytical tool/program the equation can be established in somewhat following format (Not an actual equation, just for explanation. Coefficient shall be calculated from site location to location.):

NOIM $= 7.65 - 0.53*\text{Insp} - .23*\text{Trg} + 0.67*\text{UA}$

This forms a mean for future prediction of Number of incident in month with varying value of training, Inspection and unsafe act.

In the same line analytics can be of enormous use in Industrial safety and like regression other analytics procedure liker logical regression, classification tree can be used for wide applications.

Classification Tree

A classification is a systematic approach of separating various entities into several classes. This is a decision tree based classification model, employing a binary recursive partitioning algorithm. The process initiates with the root node and keeps on branching till further split is not possible or beneficial and nodes are called a leaf.

In all the analytical processes around 70% of available data are used for training and remaining to validate the mathematical relationship. With the use of the Ginni index, Entropy, misclassification, etc data relevance to result and justify the act.

OHSAS 18001

OHSAS 18001: 1999 was developed by the OHSAS Project group, a consortium of 43 organizations from 28 countries. This consortium includes national standards bodies, registrars (certification bodies), OH & S institutes, consultants. OHSAS 18001: 2007 specifications republished as a standard in July 2007 replacing the OHSAS 18001 specification adding increased emphasis on health.

OHSAS 18001: Specification for OH&S Management Systems.

OHSAS 18002: Guidance for OH&S Management Systems.

OHSAS 18003: Criteria for auditors of OH&S Management Systems.

Benefits Envisaged:

   i.   Potential reduction in the number of accidents.

   ii. Potential reduction in downtime and associated costs

   iii. Demonstration of legal and regulatory compliance

   iv. Demonstration of commitment to stakeholders

   v.   Demonstration of innovative, forward thinking approach

   vi. Increased access to new customer and business.

   vii. Better management of risks, now and in the future.

   viii. Potential reduced public liability insurance costs.

OHSAS 18001 - Structure

OHSAS 18001 is based on:

- Hazard identification

- Risk assessment

- Determination of applicable control

OHSAS 18001 comprise of different sections as:

- General requirements

- OH&S Policy

- Planning

- Implementation and Operation

- Checking and corrective action

- Management review

ISO 45001

ISO has developed a new standard, ISO 45001, Occupational health and safety managements system requirements providing a framework to improve employee safety, reduce workplace risks and create better, safer working conditions, all over the world. This standards is in line with other safety management system such as ISO14001 and ISO 9001. It also take into account other international standards in the area such as OHSAS 18001, ILO – OHS Guidelines, various national standards and the ILO's international standards and conventions.

VIEWPOINT

- Safety in Industry, Most spoken subject and lackadaisically practiced needs to be actively supported by top management of both the partners. Adopting practices like NQA (No question asked), when implemented can improve as action followed out of fear of reporting mistakes or failure of any goal/objective can be avoided. These NQA to be analyzed annually toidentify the cause and eliminate the same.

- Using digital/mobile apps developed to implement LOTO making process error free. This shall also help making process intact, bridging any communication gap.

- Occupational Health and safety facing new challenges and unforeseen condition. Dealing with different crisis and system to address the serious issues of fire, accident with effectiveness makes a real difference. Addressing COVID 19 situation at site level is a real challenge and preparedness to dealt with situation can be display of process Efficacy.

Eg. Some basic guideline for preparedness plan for such unforeseen situation can be:

a. Forming central cell to address the crisis. Medical advisory with Medical recommendation to be communicated..

b. Maintaining communication with local health facility & arrangement for emergency services like ventilator, Quarantine facility etc.

c. Tracking for medical history of employees for diabetes, hypertension, pulmonary diseases and any medical complication to be timely reported to health centre.

d. Creating awareness and ensuring supply of required PPE ie. Masks, sanitizers and other equipment at site.

e. Social distancing to be maintained with proper attention on guest house facility and community kitchen. All common infrastructure ie. site vehicle, computers etc. to be sanitized regularly.

f. Emergency team can be shifted at site guest house restricting exposure to outside people. Shift hand over can be done at distance and even on mobile is also a good idea.

Chapter 8

Analytics in Maintenance Contracts

"If you torture the data long enough, it will confess."

– Ronald Coase

Introduction

Analytics is not new in the maintenance domain, and is being use since long with different tools to monitor the plant and equipment condition periodically, which forms the criteria to predict the future action plan leading to prescriptive analytics. Critical parameters are monitored and maintained on a real-time basis, whereas manual checklists are adopted to access the periodic status of different types of equipment in the plant. Analytics can serve a useful purpose for both service providers and customers. Earlier the use of analytics in maintenance limited to analyze the failure pattern by Paratoo analysis with the frequency of faults periodically, and minimize breakdowns (Eliminating 20% of defects causing 80% failures). But now with developed statistics employing many new software tools available, Business analytics can be widely used in different aspects of the business right from sales & Business Development, HR, KPI monitor, supply chain, vendor selection, etc.

The data handling and quality of data are now becoming a major concern. With big data efficacy of results moreover lies with input data of the entire population or sample representing the population. All models worked out with samples out of which about 70% to be used for training and the remaining 20 to 30% used for validation. Every such model shall have a definite life after which it needs to be revalidated as the model shall become irrelevant with continuously changing conditions.

Data is a cost, whereas Information is value. When data are used for important decision-making processes they have to be incorporated with different correction factors. For example, the majority of satisfied customer doesn't bother to give feedback on their own. Even when followed up for Customer satisfaction survey major chunk of matured customer rate services with good/moderate remarks in order to maintain personnel relationship and out of few are with negative always attitude, which also is of no real value. The same holds true for other surveys including employee satisfaction surveys. The outcome of these errors in surveys results in churning of customers and a high rate of employee attrition despite good scores in surveys.

Regression Analysis

It is a statistical process that enables you with some accuracy to understand the relationship between such variables as 'price and volume'. For sourcing teams this is an important and sometimes complex relationship to model as they structure deals and negotiate.

Sample Linear Regression Model

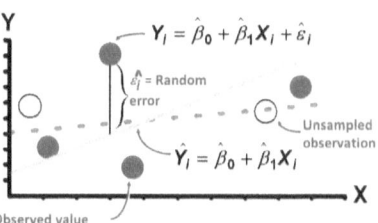

More specifically, the model helps to understand how the typical value of the dependent variable (i.e. 'price') changes when one of the independent variables is varied (i.e. 'volume'). You can use more than one independent variable meeting the specific requirement.

Regression analysis can be used for prediction and forecasting, where for the geeks out there, there is an overlap with the field of machine learning. For procurement professionals, benefits can be enlisted as;

1. **Upskilling** – Regression can be used in procurement as, it brings a new and exciting dynamic to the analytical process. This simple model can be quickly and effectively brought to bear to support professionals navigate through some of the complexities they face whilst analysing the supply market and establishing the most optimal course of action.

2. **RFP and RFI** – Once you have collected all your data on volume and price, it would be extremely useful to run this model and see if there is a tight or loose correlation in the supply market and from this decide how best to negotiate and possibly contract.

3. **Price Variation Analysis** – Much is said about price variation analysis and it is an excellent first step in the process but by including this in next step you take this analysis to a new and more valuable level. By including demand in this, you develop a powerful three dimensional predictive model from which to negotiate.

4. **Predict and/or forecast** – This first simple step is an excellent way to model and forecast/predict that given certain conditions/volume the average price you will transact at is likely to be close to the line.

Analytics for Service Provider:

Business analytics is a set of statistical and operation research techniques, artificial intelligence, information technology, and management strategies used for framing a business problem, collecting data, and analyzing the data to create value for the organization. The maintenance service provider can be considered as a small enterprise with all active functions ie. From Sales & Marketing, Supply chain, Contract management, HR, Maintenance and servicing, Logistic to Delivery. This way maintenance service organization is no different from any other organization and can use business analytics in a big way from forecasting to prescriptive analytics. Some common application in safety engineering has been discussed in the last chapter to give a general idea. The scope of analytics in the service contract is enormous with huge potential still unexplored or at a very preliminary level.

A major resource in the maintenance outsourcing business is manpower and business is run by belief and perceptions, which varies with ideology in different industries from person to person and position to position. Analytics provide better alternative than current practice of HIPO (High-income person opinion) as evident in service business.

Customer shop floor engineer may prefer particular OEM based on simple bias/perception of OEM being more resourceful for their product and technology, whereas management of OEM find it difficult to manage with an internal resource for high internal debit cost & find no quality difference with external vendor and get it done by an outside vendor. Similarly, a customer with brand loyalty for particular OEM selects the service provider with premium and surprised to see the tools & instruments used by him are of some unknown brand. These are very few examples we come across. However, we are discussing this situation on the opposite side of the tables. Even looking on the same side, the Site team stationed at the plant is more quality conscious and sincerely want to support the customer with a best possible solution with opportunity for self-development and skill up-gradation. On the other hand back-office staff is more conscious on profitability and wish to satisfy the customer with already deployed resources, and with the hierarchical upper hand it is site team on receiving side for the delivery shortcoming. This causes torsion lag between back-office management at offices and teams deployed at sites. These are few cases and the list is endless. The success probability can be considerably improved with data-driven decision-making is employed. Different regression model i.e. simple linear regression, multiple linear regression, logical regression, classification tree with associated tools like python, R, etc. can be very helpful brief of the same in different function are indicated as:

Sales & Marketing – Predictive analysis can predict the probability of occurrence of a future event such as forecasting demand for product/services, customer churn, etc. At times with many inquiries in process, predictive analysis can be effectively used to decide priority order using optimized resources with best efforts to turn maximum inquiries into order. While descriptive analytics is used to predict what has happened in past, predictive analysis is used to predict what can happen in the future. Eg. ability to predict a future event such as worldwide economic slowdown due to recent COVID-19 pandemics adversely affecting the demand in the market, which customer is likely to churn. Even in normal situations accessing a different attribute of customer behavior to match with maximum possible value delivery. A customer credit score is a popular application of logistic regression.

Costing and submitting quotation: Once it is decided to submit a quotation, the time is always a constraint. Regression analysis is a Statistical process that enables to cost with some accuracy to understand the relationship between such variables as 'price and volume'. For sourcing teams, this is an important and sometimes complex relationship to model as they structure deals and negotiate.

A simple linear regression model is developed to understand how the value of a dependent variable / KPI is associated with changes in the value of an independent variable. You can use more than one independent variable to initiate Multiple Linear Regression model building with descriptive analytics. Some examples of linear regression model can be exhibited as relationship between Order value vs Deputed team size, Service level agreement vs Supply chain cost etc.

In case of multiple variables it is necessary to assign different variables and fit into the equation as:

$$Y = \beta_0 + \beta_1 X_1 + \beta_2 X_2 + \dots \dots \beta_n X_n + \epsilon$$

In the above equation, the variable Y (dependent variable) is the Quoted price. X1, X2.... Xn are independent variables (predictor variables indicating the manpower, Supervisor to technician ratio, Competency required, Specialized services, etc.). $\beta 0$ is a constant or intercept; $\beta 1$, $\beta 2$....βn are called a partial regression coefficient corresponding to the explanatory variables X1, X2.... Xn respectively; and ϵ is error term or residual and ideally its value to approach to zero.

There should not be a high correlation between independent variables in the model (called multicollinearity). Multi – collinearity can destabilize the model and can result in incorrect estimation of the regression parameters.

Non Linear Regression Model

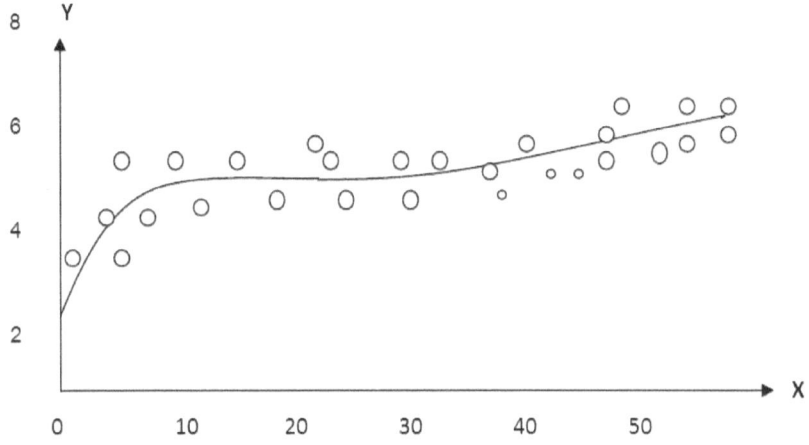

In the above example, the y can be annual order value (in Millions) and x-axis representing team strength at the site.

Service – Descriptive analytics is an important part of reporting across several industries. This enables top management to monitor Key performance indicators and decisions making. Analytical tools can be used for periodic business reviews and forecasting future revenues. Several companies use dashboards and scorecards to communicate KPIs that are relevant to them.

Supply Chain – In the usual business process, the supply chain plays a major role and an efficient supply chain is a synonym of a profitable business. Here analytics can be used to optimized use of resources and model pricing of special services with premium and discount mode.

Contract Management – Contract management forms a basis for the business and various aspects including the resource (internal & external) utilization is a key driver for profitability with customer satisfaction. Analytics can be used in decision taking in fixing up the range of the margins, group various services forming attractive service packaging at discounts to meet requirements of different customers enriching long-lasting relationships with customers. The cost of adding a new customer is always higher than retaining the existing customer and it comes with the challenge of non-familiarity. Contract performance can be monitored on moving average on the basis of KPI and other parameters with keeping eye on exponential average of performance, as it is evident that recent incidents play a crucial role in order renewal and enhancement in order value.

In the contract management space, where tens and hundreds of contracts are executed every year resulting into number of documents, analytics are key to understanding how to manage and maintain them. Here are some recommendations can be of great help as:

- Contract negotiations – how many contracts arrived for negotiation vs. how many were actually executed and how many resulted in real business:

  o Review the number of contracts that were executed the previous year to get insights on the cycle time required to close each contract.

  o Check whether you're using the same framework agreement for new business opportunities or executing new ones each time, which often leads to delays and same negotiations.

  o How many contracts never resulted into any business? Is it worth negotiating such contracts?

Understanding this kind of data will give you some excellent insights and help you reduce time and cost.

- Low value contracts – in low value contracts (for example, INR 30'0 mil (Annual value) depending on the size of the organization), how many contracts were below the threshold and how much time was spent in negotiating them? Is it worth the time? If not, you should either:

  o Advise sales not to entertain such requests.

- o   Increase the margin to cover the hidden cost of negotiation.

- o   Prepare a policy to prevent redlining on such contracts.

This will help optimize low value contracts, and reduce cost and cycle time.

- Analytics – what are the most negotiated clauses that have taken up most of your time? Can such arbitration clauses be redrafted to address the opposite party's (Government enterprises) most common issues? This will eventually reduce the negotiation cycle time and tedious approval process. Artificial intelligence (AI) and machine learning (ML) tools are equipped to give this kind of information, enabling you to tweak the language of such clauses.

- A unified approach – in large organizations where goods and services are procured or sold across geographies, contract analytics can reduce the approval and cycle time, while delivering better visibility, control, and governance. A fragmented approach may qualify an organization as low value or low risk, whereas a consolidated picture increases the chance for an organization to become a strategic partner. This represents a win-win situation for both the parties.

Overall, reporting and analytics that can answer multiple non-standard questions are a key driver in every business sphere. Contract management is no exception. This is only set to grow further and will become a much bigger part of the boardroom discussion as AI and ML tools become more mature.

HR Function: In this business, manpower being the primitive resource, making an important function. Predictive analytics can be put into use to predict attrition rate and control within a practical limit with the provision of ready to join candidates, maintaining the shortfall.

" People are the key to success or extraordinary success"

– **Azim Premji**

Performance Appraisal

Performance appraisals are notoriously unpopular with employees, managers, and HR personnel, although usually viewed as a necessary evil. There are several reasons for this attitude.

Poor Dynamic: The practice of having managers or HR personnel sit in what appears to be a position of "judgment" over employees sets up an unproductive dynamic. The worker often feels defensive, and the process may foster a sense of conflict rather than the team environment the company desires.

Inadvertent Bias: It's difficult for managers to provide honest feedback when the words are less than complimentary. Plus, tying these reviews to financial compensation can make it more difficult to rate the employee's performance without bias.

Inaccuracy: Subjectivity and accuracy are frequently a problem with the numeric rankings or ratings that periodic performance reviews rely on. The system needs standardization and reliable metrics to ensure objectivity and accuracy.

Prolonged Process: This is a lengthy, unwieldy process that requires a huge block of time from managers and HR, detracting from other important job roles and detrimentally impacting productivity.

Employees often perceive performance reviews as a process that inclines heavily towards traditional practices (Bell Curve Method), is subjective, and consumes time. If they are not satisfied with outcomes, their morale, productivity, and performance may plunge. Consequently, it may lead to high turnover. However, it is an important exercise given that it creates a high-performing culture and motivates top-performing employees. It enables the organization to identify skill gaps, develop learning and development programs, retain employees, and do succession planning.

Most organizations have realized that conventional performance review systems are outdated, do not capture real-time performance, and fail to provide timely feedback and improvement opportunities to employees.

Performance appraisal is the most difficult aspect if focused on fairness in the system, which happens to be rare as in any reward or recognition system. One could understand the seriousness of the process by simple thought one improper promotion may not improve the performance of that individual to any extent of the organization as the middle core spine of such a system will remain ineffective and de-motivated. Some examples in a big service organization are visualized as:

CASE-1: Mr. GK is a manager deployed at the back office and looks after process excellence and he is responsible for the appraisal of more than 100 employees all across different site locations. Out of those entire population of reportee, Mr. GK may be communicating with very few maybe twice or thrice a year and there is also a lot to whom he speaks only at the time of appraisal with a pre-decided mindset.

Mr. GP pushes his remarks with revision and growth in guided with organization line.

CASE-2: Mr. RH is another Manager looking after project management & supply chain with a team of reportee, sitting adjacent to his seat in office. Mr. RH maintains communication on continuous terms about various aspects of running orders, cost overrun, customer communication, etc. and the team performs more of on instruction by Mr. RH. All team members of RH before taking any initiative to take concern of Mr. RH and keep him in form of updates.

At the time of appraisal, Mr. RH calls his team member in the meeting room and asks what he has done in past one year with questions for why he behaved this way or that way, and therefore you are given increment and position as XYZ, etc. The question here is if any issue was there why not addressed at that time when communication is on daily basis. Moreover here in such situation appraisal instead of providing a fair chance within an organization. becomes the tool for justifying the management action.

Now both the cases ie. Case-1 and case-2 are contradictory, but this and many similar situations are observed at most of the workplace and more evident in service outsourcing organization.

The above case indicates the involvement of management at the micro-level and process, instead of driving excellence became ritual. Service organization with variation in industry type, the scope of work, customer approach, etc. needs to practice flexibility in place of rigid process.

A true leader is not pulled from the top by boss choice but pushed up by his subordinates and colleagues due to his undisputable position of supporting team, whenever needed. Leaders are not picked up but emerge out of adverse conditions. It is like quality assurance not about quality control.

"True leadership lies in guiding others to success. In ensuring that everyone is performing at their best, doing the work they are pledged to do, and doing it well." – Bill Owens.

HR departments is an important part of any organization and also continuously undergoing through performance and innovation process. Implementing new ideas in HR is always challenging as if applied without proper thought process and sample tests will affect the overall organization.

Inputs (only relevant) to be used for employee rating along with people like a customer, vendor, etc. to ensure all employees are fairly reviewed. Analytics with AI can be employed to develop smoothening techniques to nullify inadvertent biases due to preferences of the Area/region, qualification criteria, etc.

Example: Rating of different employees in the company in sequence from highest to lowest as in the table below. (This is just an example and, to be taken in the right perspective with industry-specific modification shall make this exercise very productive.)

S.No.	Employee	Necessary Attribute		Biased preferences		
		Technical comp	Safety Awr	Regional	Qualification	Any other
1	A	12	10	2	2	2
2	B	11	10	2	2	1
3	C	10	9.5	1	2	2
	..	..	..	1	1	1

Continued…

49	..	..	..	0	1	1
	..	..	..	0	0	1
98	y	7	5	0	0	0
100	Z	6	8	0	0	0

Scale – Necessary attribute: on the scale of 1-10, with 1 at lowest and 10 is at best.

Biased preferences: Using dummy variables 2 for positive preference, 1 for neutral and 0 for negative preferences.

Above table indicates, How biased preferences are effecting, as person with same capability is getting different rating in necessary attribute based on individual biased preferences,which can reflect in outcome of appraisal process in form of incentive, increment, promotion or other advantages/disadvantages and shall lead to deteriorating work culture.

Schematic Diagram with outliers and Confidence level

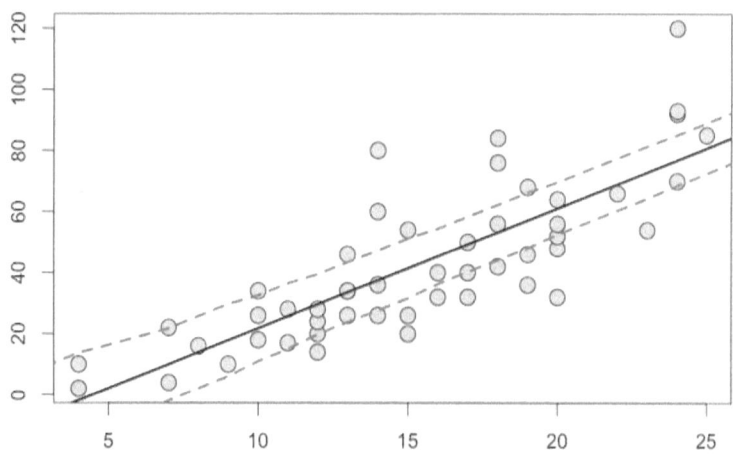

Now looking into the above example we can correlate between necessary attribute and biased preferences and their effect on outliers. Using proper smoothening techniques, with nullifying biased preferences the system effectiveness is expected to improve.

Even an increase in confidence level, looking into job requirements can raise the σ (SD) include additional outliers within standard deviations.

Appraisal process with multiple inputs to nullify the bias can be a good choice. However there should not be a high correlation between independent variables in the model (called multicollinearity). Feedback from other supervisors doesn't serves the purpose if influenced by same manager, which will again develop high correlation between independent variable making regression model unstable and ineffective.

Additionally, there are lots of variance in form of Industry type, customer behavior, etc. As a general rule operation in moderate size is considered to be ok, whereas Industries (Both very large and very small offers different challenges). These all types of variants to be taken into account and analytics can be of great help to match the suitability of employees to its site characteristic rather than making random moments to fulfill manpower count to meet commitments.

As discussed, with wide variance in a customer in terms of industry, competency, preferences, etc. there comes to be a rare possibility of a team member being a misfit in such an organization except in a condition of indiscipline or refuse to work stretching the rejection limit to very low.

Quality: Six Sigma and its problem – solving methodology DMAIC (Define, Measure, Analysis, Improve, and Control) are frequently used in any process improvement process. The same is applicable in the maintenance process. 4σ is within acceptable industrial standard. As it is plotted on a normal distribution curve and limited to a maximum of 6σ, beyond which curve follows asymptote and the cost to maintain quality approaches to the higher side.

One of the primary objectives of six sigma is improving customer satisfaction by ensuring defect – free delivery of products and services. A frequently quoted example of six sigma methodology in India is Mumbai Dabbawalas. Every morning in Mumbai, about 5,000 Dabbawalas (Lunch box delivery men;) collect about 200,000 dabbas (Lunch boxes) from houses in various suburbs in Mumbai, carry them on the suburban trains, and deliver them to various offices, colleges, and school in and around Mumbai so that its citizen can eat fresh and hygienic homemade food (Thomke and Sinha, 2013). In 2017, the customer were charged approximately INR

500/ – to 900/ – (around USD 8 to 12) per month for this service. The most amazing fact about the massive logistic operation is the dabbawalas almost never fail to deliver the lunch boxes to their rightful owners. Forbes magazine reported that the reliability of this service in the delivery of dabbas to their rightful owners meets Six Sigma standards. The defect rate (failure to deliver a lunch box to its rightful owner) of the dabbawalas is approximately 1 in 16 million transactions, putting them in enviable position in six sigma scale of performance is 5.286 precisely.

Data at a macro – level can be classified as structured and unstructured data. Structured data means the data is described in a matrix form with labeled rows and columns. Any data that is not originally in matrix form with labeled rows and columns is an unstructured data. For example, e-mails, textual data, images, etc. Machine-generated data such as images generated by satellite, Magnetic resonance imaging (MRI), thermography are few examples of unstructured data. Before building up of any analytics model, unstructured data has to be converted into structured data.

Analytics for Outsourcing Decision Taking

The decision concerning maintenance outsourcing was traditionally executed using cost-based decision models. However, the dramatic change in the way maintenance function is viewed had challenged the validity of this approach. Today, maintenance outsourcing decision is analyzed in a different way, taking into account the complex and extended set of (tangible and/or intangible) strategic factors. An analytical multi attributable decision method named AHP (Analytical hierarchy process) deployed as a means to encourage managers to appraise the range and complexities of the issue that needs to be considered when making a decision concerning maintenance outsourcing.

Cost of poor quality: Cost of poor quality (CopQ) measures the cost of resources that are used for activities that exist as a result of process deficiencies. The CopQ is the sum of conformance cost and non-conformance cost, where conformance cost is the cost related to the prevention of poor quality and non – conformance cost is the cost resulting from the poor quality of product and/or service failure.

In terms of maintenance outsourcing, a set of potential and attractive benefits can be reached such as to increase labor productivity, to reduce maintenance costs, to focus in-house personnel on "core" activities, to improve environmental performances, to obtain specialist skills not available in house, to improve work quality, etc.. However, outsourcing also involves a set of drawbacks that must be taken into account by the customer:

- loss of control and loss of a learning source, because an internal activity is externalised;
- loss of knowledge of the plant;
- possible dependencies on the supplier;
- variations in the quality of the product given to the customer; and
- problems among personnel, since they lose their functions

Of course, the magnitude of these benefits and risks depends on the qualifications of the supplier and on the selected type of outsourcing contract (i.e. the number and type of maintenance activities outsourced). This is the principal reason for applying methodological foundations when maintenance services are supplied.

It must be stated that the outsourcing of certain functions or services should not be considered as the synonym for granted success. Strategic factors that can ensure a higher possibility of success in the process of moving from centralised maintenance management to the outsourcing of certain services can be identified in:

- the strategic analysis – to this, in particular, is demanded the evaluation of the actual feasibility of the entire project, on the basis of the existing corporate constraints;
- the research for those activities that should be managed in outsourcing and the selection of the providers for their realisation; and

- the management of relationships between service provider and customer – this requires that the corporation already owns new managerial capabilities, not necessarily pre-existent, and the definition of suitable monitoring and evaluation procedures.

The real capacity of a corporation to move from a centralised management to the outsourcing practices must be measured on the basis of an accurate analysis aimed to determine:

- which are the internal services to externalise;

- the real capacities and the eventual restrictions of the local market to successfully conduct co-operative agreements; and

- the effectiveness, in terms of costs, of the outsourcing process to reach the competitive advantages previously mentioned.

Therefore, the management should measure the effective presence of possible causes of domestic problems, that may be difficult to eradicate, and the conditions by which the outsourcing activities may allow a better mix of quality, costs, and service level with respect to the internal solution. For these reasons, an appropriate feasibility study should be executed.

During the feasibility study, the maintenance staff should solve a set of complex and critical decisional problems generally based on a large amount of tangible/intangible factors that must be analysed and considered:

Evaluate Company Readiness to Outsource

Prior to starting the outsourcing program, the company should objectively evaluate its actual situation with respect to some critical issues. Briefly, maintenance staff should adequately review internal structure, processes and management procedures, personnel capabilities, and their responsiveness to changes and innovations. Doing so, a significant picture of the overall ability to manage the outsourcing program could be drawn and, at the same time, the company's readiness to outsource maintenance activities could be somehow quantified.

Define Activities to Outsource

The choice of the activities to be externalised represents another important decision to be faced at the very early stages of the outsourcing program. Generally, "non-core "competencies are all good candidates for outsourcing, being standard, well defined and repetitive activities (such as, for example, repair of generic and common equipment's, electrical and electronic parts and plant overhauls). Besides, many of them are adequately performed by a growing number of specialized suppliers available in the marketplace, with interesting costs and quality rates. In this case, the risk of losing expertise and know – how is very little, while, on the other hand, in-house maintenance personnel can concentrate on critical and valuable technical topics and other business analytics with focus on data driven decision making.

Select a Contractor

To maximize the potential advantages and, at the same time, to minimize the risks deriving from the adoption of outsourcing policies, an extremely important role is covered by the selection of the right supplier. Thus, it is necessary to develop the selection criteria and the benchmarking activities to evaluate and analyse their capabilities. For example:

- geographical position (i.e. local contractor presence);
- the perceived quality of goods and services;
- contractor flexibility;
- technical excellence (i.e. proven staff and management);
- leadership;
- plant-specific know-how and experience; and
- low price.

These are some good examples of performance factors that may be used for this aim. In addition, emphasis to be laid on outsourcing arrangements with suppliers bringing "partnership philosophy" making it a successful model of operation. In other words, it is crucial to obtain a spirit of co-operation and mutual understanding to sustain an ongoing that benefits both parties.

Monitor the Contractor's Performance

The outsourcing contractor assumes greater responsibility for the successful performance of the function being outsourced, sharing not only rewards but risks as well. A fundamental aspect for the adoption of outsourcing policies is strictly joined to a clear and unambiguous definition of responsibilities so that it can be possible to establish a link between the performances of an item with the maintenance activities effectiveness, both when the control activities are performed by the customer or by the service provider. From this point of view, it becomes extremely important to define a system of performance indicators, usually linked with quality, quantity, and costs. Quality measures are usually linked to the time necessary to restore the equipment. Quantity refers to the commitment of the service provider to assure the required services. Finally, costs should be used to evaluate how much the investments for adjusting and enhancing the maintenance service reflect into a measurable reduction of all those costs that can be related to the disservice following a failure. The most commonly used measures of contractor's performance are:

- price/cost;
- equipment availability (e.g., MTBF);
- safety and environmental performances (e.g., average number of incidents);
- on-time performance (e.g., MTTR);
- work quality/rework; and
- amount of work.

The approaches proposed in the past were concern with the development of decision making systems during the critical and complex decision problems that a manager encounters in an outsourcing project are frequently based on a list of detailed steps and considerations that the decision-maker should carefully follow for a successful implementation of an outsourcing effort. No numerical/statistical methodologies were generally employed. Here it is an attempt to present an analytical approach, able to be used as a decision-making tool during the choice of the most appropriate type of outsourcing contract. It is evident that the selection of a particular contract implies the choice of the activities that management decides to outsource. The procedure is based on a well-known multi-criteria decision technique named the analytic hierarchy process.

Reasons for Using Contract Maintenance Services (A Complex Decision Problem)

A detailed list of reasons for using maintenance contractors to be discussed vividly within the organisation with the active participation of maintenance, procurement, and contract cell representative with some points enlisted as hereunder:

- increase labour productivity;
- reduce maintenance costs;
- focus in-house personnel on "core" activities ;
- reduce management effort;
- obtain specialist skills not available in-house;
- level fluctuations in workload;
- increase access to specialist equipment;
- improve equipment uptime/performance;
- reduce risk;
- improve work quality;
- reduce influence of trade unions;
- improve environmental performance; and
- keep pace with rapidly changing technology.

It is interesting to note that even when starting as cost reduction initiatives, outsourcing is not just a costing exercise but it has a strategic dimension that must be carefully considered and analysed. In other words, the role of outsourcing is not only a cost-saving method but also a part of the overall management strategy to focus on core competitiveness. For these reasons, making outsourcing decisions requires deeper analysis than most companies realise.

Unfortunately, single cost-based decision processes remain the most used approaches by maintenance managers for making outsourcing decisions. The cost dimension may be sufficient if maintenance is strictly considered a support functional cost center. But, following the new maintenance strategies such as TPM, if maintenance is considered a stand-alone business unit, different approaches are necessary.

Any proposal for a manufacturing outsourcing decision usually comprises of three main key aspects and needs to be analysed:

1. The quantifiable (costs, investments, revenues, etc.) and non-quantifiable contextual factors (strategic interest, confidentiality, the stability of employment, etc.), associated with the context of the particular process that is being considered for outsourcing. These factors can be internal and/or external to the specific activity under analysis and are scored and ranked by using a Likert scale from 1 to 5.

2. The strategic and structural implications associated with the company's decision. Based on a set of questions proposed by different stakeholders within the organization, a guideline framed to help organization consider the structural aspects associated with the decision and, in particular, to focus on how integrated the organization should be (e.g. can the corporate culture be changed? How long will the process be viable? etc.).

3. The costs associated with the process or activity under review.

Outsourcing should be viewed as a long-term measure when deciding what to outsource, selecting providers, cultivating an outsourcing relationship, and making other outsourcing decisions. In the field of human resources departments, the author proposed a five-step decision process. It is interesting to underline, in this context, how the last step is represented by a balance of the potential effects deriving from a particular choice of outsourcing level. This is the most critical step in the decision process, considering that the different variables analyzed will head to different directions and the management will have a tough time balancing the factors. In other words, the final outsourcing decision process can be represented as a complex multi-attribute decision problem.

A stepwise approach is presented as a framework to outsource in a systematic way, addressing the key issues around objectives, readiness, alternatives, proposals, and negotiations. The six steps can be briefly described with the following questions:

- Does outsourcing make sense?
- Are your objectives achievable?
- Is the organisation ready?
- What are the outsourcing alternatives?
- How is the request for the outsourcing proposal structured?
- What are the negotiating tactics?

With emerging data analytics, a new graphical method to make maintenance outsourcing decisions, also defining what activities are better to outsource. The model introduces not only the cost aspect but also a strategic dimension that lets maintenance managers focus on broader, long-term objectives as well as short-term costs issues. Based on a "cost index diagram", the departmental cost gaps, suitably correlated with the department's relative budget, appear again to be the leading factor. In addition, a second diagram permits to correlate the cost results with the strategic concept named "core competency". Core competency is defined as a set of skills critical to maintaining in-house for the plant to be successful. In this way, all aspects of maintenance activities are analysed in a critical manner and ranked by carefully isolating the cause and effect of each process.

Data Driven Decision Making

Data-driven decision making (DDDM) is a process that involves collecting data based on measurable goals or KPIs, analyzing patterns and facts from these insights, and utilizing them to develop strategies and activities that benefit the business in a number of areas.

Fundamentally, data-driven decision making means working towards key business goals by leveraging verified, analyzed data rather than merely shooting in the dark.

However, to extract genuine value from your data, it must be accurate as well as relevant to your aims. Collecting, extracting, formatting, and analyzing insights for enhanced data-driven decision making in business was once an all-encompassing task, which naturally delayed the entire data decision making process.

The qualitative analysis focuses on data that isn't defined by numbers or metrics such as interviews, videos, Documentation, Housekeeping, and Quality. Qualitative data analysis is based on observation rather than measurement. Here, it's crucial to coding the data to ensure that items are grouped together methodically as well as intelligently.

Quantitative data analysis focuses on numbers and statistics. The median, standard deviation, and other descriptive stats play a pivotal role here. This type of analysis is measured rather than observed. Both qualitative and quantitative data should be analysed to make smarter data-driven business decisions.

The importance of data in decision lies in consistency and continual growth. It enables companies to create new business opportunities, generate more revenue, predict future trends, optimize current operational efforts, and produce actionable insights. That way, you stand to grow and evolve your empire over time, making your organization more adaptable as a result. The digital world is in a constant state of flux, and to move with the ever-changing landscape around you, you must leverage data to make more informed and powerful data-driven business decisions.

A. Enhanced Data Driven Decision Making Strategy

Finally, here are few practical tips and takeaways for better data driven decision making in business. By the end, you'll be sure of the importance of making these kinds of decisions.

a) Guard against your biases

Much of the mental work we do is unconscious, which makes it difficult to verify the logic we use when we make a decision. We can even be guilty of seeing the data we wish was there instead of what's really in front of us. This is one of the ways a good team can help. Running your decisions by a competent party who doesn't share (or even know) your biases is an invaluable step.

Working with a team who knows the data you are working with opens the door to helpful and insightful feedback. Democratizing data empowers all people, regardless of their technical skills, to access it and help make informed decisions. Often this is done through innovative dashboard software, visualizing once complicated tables and graphs in such ways that more people can initiate good data-driven business decisions.

With more people understanding the data at play, you'll have an opportunity to receive more credible feedback. The proof is in the numbers. A 2010 McKinsey study (which is helpful to read even today) of more than 1,000 major business investments showed that when organizations worked at reducing the effect of bias in their decision-making processes, they achieved returns up to 7% higher. When it comes to data-driven decision making (DDDM), reducing bias and letting numbers speak for themselves make all the difference.

Overcoming biased behavior – An Approach

Simple Awareness – Everyone is biased, but being aware that bias exists can affect your decision-making can help limit their impact. This remains more evident in maintenance, as people in a different industry, set up with different backgrounds are biased with a different thought process. Even by employing AI & smoothness technique for biases as discussed in Employee appraisal, makes the conscious effect of bias eradication

Collaboration – Your colleagues can help keep you in check since it is easier to see biases in others than in yourself. Bounce decisions off other people and be aware of biased behavior in the boardroom.

Seeking out Conflicting Information – Ask the right questions to yourself and others to recognize your biases and remove them from your decision process.

By eliminating bias, you open yourself up to discovering more opportunities. Getting rid of preconceived notions and really studying the data can alert you to insights that can truly change your bottom line. Remember, business intelligence shouldn't only be about avoiding losses, but winning gains.

b) Define objectives

To get the most out of your data teams, companies should define their objectives before beginning their analysis. Set a strategy to avoid following the hype instead of the needs of your business and define clear Key Performance Indicators (KPIs). Although there are various KPI examples you could choose from, don't overdo it and concentrate on the most important ones within your industry.

c) Gather data now

Gathering the right data is as crucial as asking the right questions. For smaller businesses or start-ups, data collection should begin on day one. Jack Dorsey, co-creator and founder of Twitter, shared this learning with Stanford. "For the first two years of Twitter's life, we were flying blind... we're basing everything on intuition instead of having a good balance between intuition and data... so the first thing I wrote for Square is an admin dashboard. We have a very strong discipline to log everything and measure everything". That being said, and done, implementing a business dashboard culture in your company is a key component to manage properly the tidal waves of data you will collect.

d) Find the unresolved questions

Once your strategy and goals are set, you will then need to find the questions in need of an answer, so that you reach these goals. Asking the right data analysis questions helps teams focus on the right data, saving time and money. In the examples earlier in this article, both Walmart and Google had very specific questions, which greatly improved the results. That way, you can focus on the data you really need, and from bluntly collecting everything "just in case" you can move to "collecting this to answer that".

e) Find the data needed to solve these questions

Among the data you have gathered, try to focus on your ideal data, which will help you answer the unresolved questions defined at the previous stage. Once it is identified, check if you already have this data collected internally, or if you need to set up a way to collect it or acquire it externally.

f) Analyze and understand

That may seem obvious, but we have to mention it: after setting the frame of all the questions to answer and the data collection, you then need to read through it to extract meaningful insights and analytical reports that will lead you to make data driven business decisions. In fact, user feedback is a useful tool for carrying out more in-depth analyses into the customer experience and extracting actionable insights. To do this successfully, it's important to have context. For example, if you want to improve conversions in the purchasing funnel, understanding why visitors are dropping off is going to be a critical insight. By analysing the responses in the open comments of your feedback form (within this funnel), you will be able to see why they're not successful in the checkout and optimize your website accordingly.

g) Don't be afraid to revisit and re-evaluate

Our brains leap to conclusions and are reluctant to consider alternatives; we are particularly bad at revisiting our first assessments. A friend who is a graphic designer once told me that he would often find himself stuck towards the end of a project. He was committed to the direction he had chosen and did not want to scrap it. He was invested, for the wrong reasons. Without fail, when this happened he would have to start all over again to see the misstep that got him stuck. Invariably, the end product was light-years better reworked than if he had cobbled together a solution from the first draft.

Verifying data and ensuring you are tracking the right metrics can help you step out of your decision patterns. Relying on team members to have a perspective and to share it can help you see the biases. But do not be afraid to step back and to rethink your decisions. It might feel like a defeat for a moment, but to succeed, it's a necessary step. Understanding where we might have gone wrong and addressing it right away will produce more positive results than if we are to wait and see what happens. The cost of waiting to see what happens is well documented...

h) Present the data in a meaningful way

Digging and gleaning insights is nice, but managing to tell your discoveries and convey your message is better. You have to make sure that your acumen doesn't remain untapped and dusty, and that it will be used for future decision making. With the help of a great data visualization software, you don't need to be an IT crack to build and customize a powerful online dashboard that will tell your data story and assist you, your team, and your management to make the right data-driven business decisions.

i) Set measurable goals for decision making

After you have your question, your data, your insights, then comes the hard part: decision making. You need to apply the findings you got to the business decisions, but also ensure that your decisions are aligned with the company's mission and vision, even if the data are contradictory. Set measurable goals to be sure that you are on the right track... and turn data into action!

j) Continue to evolve your data driven business decisions

This is often overlooked, but it's incredibly important nonetheless: you should never stop examining, analyzing, and questioning your data-driven decisions. In our hyper-connected digital age, we have more access to data than ever before. To extract real value from this wealth of insights, it's vital to continually refresh and evolve your business goals based on the landscape moving around you.

B. Data Driven Decision – Errors to be Avoided

At this point, the importance of data in decision making is clear. But while understanding the dynamics of data-driven business decisions and exploring real-world data-driven decision making in business is consistent, results-driven, and centered on your goals at all times.

a) Quality of the data

First and foremost, the main reason usually invoked is data quality. Data quality is the condition of a set of qualitative or quantitative variables, that should be "fit for [its] intended uses in operations, decision making and planning", according to an article written by author Thomas C. Redmann. A good data quality management (from the acquisition to the maintenance, from the disposition to the distribution processes in place within an organization) is also key in the future use of such data. Collecting and gathering are only good if well managed and exploited afterward, otherwise, the assets' potential remains untouched and useless.

b) Over-Reliance on past experience

Over-reliance on past experience can kill any business. If you are always looking behind you, there is a real chance of missing what is in front. So often, business leaders are hired because of their previous experiences, but environments and markets change and the same tricks may not work next time. One of the most cited examples of this is Dick Fuld, who saved Lehman after the LTCM crisis. Ten years later he pulled out the same bag of tricks and, as the Wall Street Journal reports, "the experience he was relying on was not the same as this massive housing-driven collapse." The recent crisis was much more complex. Environments and markets constantly change and, in order to be a successful manager, one must combine past experiences with current data.

c) Going with your gut and cooking the data

While some managers naturally go with their instinct, there is a significant portion who first trust their gut, then persuade their researchers or an external consultancy to produce reports that confirm the decision that they already made.

d) Cognitive biases

Cognitive biases are tendencies to make decisions based on limited information, or on lessons from past experiences that may not be relevant to the current situation. Cognitive bias occurs every day, in some way, in every decision we make. These biases can influence business leaders to ignore solid data and go with their assumptions, instead. Here are a few examples of cognitive biases commonly seen:

Confirmation bias – Business leaders tend to favor information that confirms the beliefs they already have, right or wrong.

Cognitive inertia – The inability to adapt to new environmental conditions and stick to old beliefs despite data proving otherwise.

Group Thinks – The desire to be part of the group by siding with the majority, regardless of evidence or motives to support.

Optimism Bias – Making decisions based on the belief that the future will be much better than the past.

Managers need to recognize that we are biased in every situation. There is no such thing as objectivity. The good news is that there are ways to overcome biased behavior.

As a result, these businesses identify business opportunities and predict future trends more accurately, generating more revenue and fostering greater growth through data decision making.

C. Data-Driven Decision – E.g. of Successful References

Now that we've gained a clearer understanding of what it means to make a data-driven decision as well as the importance of data-driven decision making, we're going to delve into 3 inspiring data-driven decision making examples.

a) Google

One of the most notable examples of data-driven decision making comes from search colossus Google, according to an article written on smartdatacollective.com. Startups are famous for disbanding hierarchies, and Google was curious as to whether having managers actually mattered.

To answer the question, data scientists at Google looked at performance reviews and employee surveys from the managers' subordinates (qualitative data). The analysts plotted the information on a graph and determined that managers were generally perceived as good. They went a step further and split the data into the top and bottom quartiles, then ran regressions. These tests showed large differences between the best and worst managers in terms of team productivity, employee happiness, and employee turnover. Good managers make Google more money and create happier employees, but what makes a good manager at Google?

Again, the analysts reviewed data from the "Great Manager Award" scores, in which employees could nominate managers who did an exceptional job. The employees had to provide examples explaining exactly what made the manager so great. Managers from the top and bottom quartiles were also interviewed to round out the data set. Google's analysis found the top 8 behaviors that make a great manager at Google and 3 that don't. They revised their management training, incorporating the new findings, continuing the Great Manager Award, and implementing a twice-yearly feedback survey.

b) Walmart

Walmart used a similar process when it came to emergency merchandise in preparation for Hurricane Frances in 2004, as The NY Times reported. Executives wanted to know the types of merchandise they should stock before the storm. Their analysts mined records of past purchases from other Walmart stores under similar conditions, sorting a terabyte of customer history to decide which goods to send to Florida (quantitative data). It turns out that, in times of natural disasters, Americans turn to strawberry Pop-Tarts and beer. Linda M. Dillon, Walmart's CIO at the time, explained:

"By predicting what's going to happen, instead of waiting for it to happen... trucks filled with toaster pastries and six-packs were soon speeding down Interstate 95 toward Walmarts in the path of Frances." Walmart's analysts not only kept Floridians pleasantly buzzed on beer and Pop-Tarts during the storm, but also created profits by anticipating demand since most of the products sold quickly.

c) Southwest Airlines

A data-driven decision holds an incredible level of value across all industries, but one sector widely-known to benefit from such insights is the airline industry.

Southwest Airlines executives utilized targeted customer data to gain a deeper understanding of what new services would be most popular with customers as well as most profitable. In doing so, the airline discovered that by observing and analyzing their consumers' online behaviors and activities, it could provide different segments of customers the best rates for their needs in addition to an exemplary level of customer experience (CX). As a direct result of this emphasis on data-driven decisions, Southwest Airlines has seen its customer base, as well as its brand loyalty, grow steadily year after year. Maintaining machines and equipment at peak performance levels can be a constant battle. Many asset managers are turning to predictive maintenance as a tactic to take the guesswork out of asset upkeep.

By using data and analytics, predictive maintenance helps asset managers determine the best time to replace equipment and send in the engineers, which is usually just before complete failure occurs, but not unnecessarily early.

Shifting to this approach can require a change in mindset and adapting your usual work habits to new technology; once you've decided to take the leap, here are four steps to take for a smooth transition.

Assets Suitability to Maintenance Model – Decision Making

Allowing critical assets to run to failure can exacerbate issues, pose a danger to operators, and result in increased downtime; therefore, it is best to avoid this strategy for your most important assets.

But which equipment will benefit from a predictive approach, and which should you replace as needed on a time-based or reactive-maintenance model?

To determine this, you must first find out what information has been and is currently being collected for each asset. For example, do you have monitoring information, such as sensor data, that can be analysed? Do you have an inspection plan? Have you recorded all maintenance history? From this information, you can determine how critical each asset is and whether you have enough information for adequate analysis.

Data is crucial to foreseeing potential issues, so assets with plentiful, good-quality inspection and sensor data, along with past maintenance information, are ideal for predictive maintenance.

From here, you can put together a plan that allows you to increase the intervals between maintenance events and reduce your overall costs, as well as sustain and improve plant reliability.

Asset Monitoring – An Approach

Understanding the current condition of your equipment alone is not enough. Only by combining real-time data from sensors—the more the better—with historical trends and other data sets, such as age, inspection records, usage, and output, can you build a full picture of the health of each asset.

Typically, you can use existing sensors for this kind of monitoring. Occasionally, however, the sensors installed in the factory are inadequate to anticipate all the failure modes. In this case, you may need to add additional ones, such as partial discharge or flux probes.

It's important to be able to make sense of monitoring data and look for very specific indicators to recognize patterns. For example, if a temperature on a device increases suddenly, then you know there's a problem. Similarly, if a particular signal stays within a normal range, but is still behaving differently from the way it usually behaves, you should investigate the new pattern.

The value from this pattern-recognition approach lies in taking that information and drawing a conclusion about what's happening in the physical world. Over time, this kind of subtle monitoring allows you to notice sooner when a particular component has an issue.

Finding the Right Partner for Your Plant

If you're making big investments in predictive maintenance and sensor analysis, it's important to make sure you get the most out of it.

As an asset manager, you may decide to do analysis and monitoring in-house, which requires building your own maintenance and data center and training your engineers to study and interpret the data. You can also outsource that work to a partner who specializes in it.

A partner does all the analysis for you, using specialized tools and expertise, and then informs you when a problem occurs. Often, selecting the right strategy and partner is the key to a successful predictive-maintenance plan.

Furthermore, when monitoring becomes more important and the technology more sophisticated, outsourcing to a specialist has several advantages. But what should you look for in a partner?

Typically, partners will stay in touch periodically, giving you daily, weekly, or monthly updates, so practical issues such as time zone and language are important. However, finding a company that knows what matters to your operation is paramount.

For the best results, any partner you choose should have a large data set and monitoring fleet, excellent technical expertise, and an expansive portfolio of analytics. They should also be able to help you carefully develop a reliable maintenance strategy, which may involve helping you select which assets to put on your plan.

You'll be working closely with any partner you choose, so make sure the people behind the technology are the right fit for your organization. While vetting partners, take the time to ask questions about the companies' culture, response times, and preferred communication channels.

Maintain Good Inventory Management

Managing spare parts and supplies can be a challenge—one that's exacerbated when dealing with many different types of equipment. Spares can also be expensive and a significant segment of your maintenance budget. Therefore, lastly, managing your spare-part inventory is a good idea to improve the success and cost-effectiveness of predictive maintenance. Transferring to a new maintenance approach can seem daunting initially. But once you find the right partner, together you can plan how to move forward. Remember to discuss what assets to monitor, what data is needed, if any additional monitoring equipment is required, and how to approach inventory management. Besides this, all that's necessary is a fresh mindset and a willingness to take a new approach to improve your plant.

VIEWPOINT

- Analytics can be used to evaluate life time revenue for customer and customer churn up. E.g. The costing and pricing plays very important role as printer manufacturer maintains monopoly and supply printer cartridge at premium price in market. But one should understand everything has some life and if premium continues to be high than premium does not sustain as customer does not find value in it and give space to cheaper substitute or a competition, may be of inferior quality. That's how ink refilling entered into market.

The manufacturer in above case could have conducted predictive analysis for product costing as premium for certain period than discounted modeling (may be replacement of old un-damaged cartridge) and finally switching to refilling model with pre-decided life time revenues limiting space for competitors, adding up revenue life.

Chapter 9

Maintenance Outsourcing – Service Provider Perspective

"Contractors always pursue large profit, the customer – a high quality end product in due time and at a lower cost. This struggle never ends, but this is natural".

– **Vladimir Putin**

Introduction

Once walking through a medical/health store for some medicines, find many brands of antioxidants displayed in a rack for health products. Suddenly I got through thought that on one hand oxygen is required for a human being for basic survival and on another hand antioxidants are marketed as health product. Antioxidants are expected to delay decay in the system, where oxygen act as a catalyst.

Maintenance in the manufacturing industry are like antioxidant improving the asset lifecycle cost and for service provider business it is oxygen. In other words, effective maintenance impacts the bottom line as the cost for the customer and top line for the service provider as total revenues from sales respectively. The entire business is about scaling between Top Line (Service Provider) and Bottom line (Customer).

In the case of Service providers, being OEM for a product will also aim for additional business on product sales with the opportunity to improve the top line. But it is also noticed in most organizations with large product mix and multiple sales team with everyone busy in chasing big targets i.e. small orders are leftover and are not properly addressed leading to customer un-satisfaction. This low value may vary from a few hundred Rupees to few lacs Rupees and is classified as depending upon the size of the organization.

I strongly feel, sales target in any organization shall not be fixed in terms of sales value only but order nos. also i.e. Tgt of 40'0 mi with an order of 40 nos. This will ensure value may be achieved by few orders but small orders will also be executed with equal importance. On one hand sales target in value will make the company rich, on other hand even timely execution of small orders shall enhance customer satisfaction level. This will not only add to customer span but also increase market penetration.

Analytics for Service Provider

As evident from any service provider perspective, all managers are always under extreme pressure from all three directions i.e. immediate management for the continuous flowing revenue stream, customer for better service & Employee for career growth and opportunities. Maintaining balance among three is a real challenge but most of the time end up with over-commitment to all causing turbulent situations, similar to three-phase asymmetrical fault as friends from an electrical engineering background would be quite familiar with.

This sometimes reminds me of folk story of " Rumpelstiltskin" read in childhood where miller (Service provider) who gets his daughter (Site deputed employee) in trouble falsely telling the King (Customer) she can spin straw into gold. Unfortunately, Rumpelstiltskin who helped the girl in spinning gold does not exist in real world.

Maintenance outsourcing is increasing competitive business in the market with multiple service offerings. Now with a lot of manufacturing organizations employing reverse auction process for finalizing contract the contract price has become a driving factor for such decisions. As a service provider also it becomes necessary to understand the customer business and requirement to ensure business profitability with quality delivery. Here analytics can be widely used right from customer credit rating before offer submission to fixing up the maintenance schedule. Analytics can be used to find out an appropriate mix of qualification, Industry Experience (General & Relevant) to fix up the eligibility criteria for different categories of people to be deployed at the site. Even a mathematical model can be used to work out the preliminary cost using different coefficients for Industry type, Supervisor/worker ratio, Competency required as variables. Even KPI to be analyzed with an appropriate mathematical model to be formulated establishing an association between final KPI and other predictive variables.

Inventory Management at Customer Scope

Once the Maintenance team deployed at a site, many activities commence in parallel to suitable preparedness for upcoming challenges after the commencement of the contract.

Spare parts & Service planning –

Perhaps the most challenging aspect of initiating Maintenance plans in coordination with customer procurement in order to forecast demand. Asset maintenance, being the demand driver, presents two types of demand in the MRO supply chain—Planned and Unplanned. Planned demand arises out of planned preventive/predictive maintenance plans, corrective repairs identified from preventive/predictive inspections, shutdown plans, and field change orders where material needs can be seen in advance. Unplanned demand arises from breakdowns and other unplanned maintenance. Whereas demand visibility provides an opportunity for the MRO supply chain to provide needed material in a timely and efficient manner, the demand is not visible if the plans are not developed in the ERP or CMMS system or if maintenance personnel conduct planning or work order management manually outside the associated system without capturing the needed information. Reduced visibility of demand adversely impacts inventory management and sourcing processes, leading to higher costs throughout the supply chain.

Challenges in Inventory management

Difficulty Managing Inventory MRO inventories are characterized by large numbers of SKUs, different attributes, and highly variable demand ranging from rarely used items to high-volume items. Criticality and demand variability further complicate the inventory planning process. All these factors require highly skilled resources for planning and to set the appropriate stocking policy. Few ERP or CMMS systems come with dynamic inventory planning features, adding to the difficulty of inventory planning. Due to these planning difficulties, the following problems often arise:

Suboptimal inventories: Ranging from too high for some parts to unavailability or low inventory for others

High inventory levels greater than industry benchmarks: Typically, 0.3 to 1.5% of Replacement Asset Value (RAV) depending on the industry

Lower service levels

Higher level of non-moving or obsolete parts

Assets under-maintained for longer intervals due to unavailable parts.

The site deployed team needs to align with the customer procurement process for and support from the identification of spares, order, vendor selection and follow up to receipt of material. Some challenges at customer end can be as follows:

Fragmented Supply Base

Fragmented supply base across categories is another challenge. With multiple locations and decentralized procurement processes, the supply base is inevitably even more fragmented. There may be multiple entries or codes for the same vendor, making it difficult to monitor and manage spend across vendors.

Complex and Non-Uniform Procurement Processes

The value of MRO materials varies significantly, as does the associated procurement and approval processes. It has been frequently observed that approval and procurement processes vary widely between sites within the same organization. Complexity in procurement processes increases the internal lead time, which increases the need for safety stock of materials and adds to purchase order processing costs.

Master Data Management

Plant master data, one of the most critical elements of any plant maintenance system, must be managed effectively. Businesses assume that their data is accurate with respect to the simple identification of parts and assets. Unfortunately, this is often not the case. Every storeroom has duplicate parts—the same parts with different identifications. Such duplication promotes excess holdings and can also create apparent part shortages when a one-part name is needed but not held—and conversely, the same part is on-hand but under a different ID. One of the initial steps of any MRO optimization initiative is data cleansing. To maximize return on investment, assets, and inventory data must be accurate and in a standardized form. Companies should begin by building databases that ensure the integrity and accuracy of inventory information. With accurate and reliable database information, companies can maintain lower inventory levels and create data-driven purchasing. Organizations should also review the existing master data management processes and systems, apply discipline to the entire process, and focus on improving the quality of master data for assets, suppliers, parts catalogs, part categorization, maintenance task lists, and part and asset BOM linkages on an ongoing basis. If data is being managed in multiple locations and systems, then consideration should be given to moving this function to a centralized location.

Benefits of centralizing master data management include increased accuracy and standardization of the data set and accountability of the data team. Since better data helps eliminate costs and improve profits, how do companies improve their MRO item data? It may seem like an overwhelming task, but by breaking the task into defined, manageable steps, it can be achieved.

Data Cleansing

Cleansing and structuring the data is the first step. Many MRO item descriptions are stored as unstructured, free-form text. Converting these text-based descriptions into structured data based on a set of standard modifiers provides many benefits:

Structured data forms the baseline information for developing a robust MRO catalog

Duplicate data can start to be recognized and reduced

Structured data is more readily searched, allowing technicians and purchasing agents to find parts quickly

Enterprise Resource Planning (ERP) and Enterprise Asset Management (EAM) systems are able to make better use of structured data

Data Standardization

Once the data is in a structured format, it can be standardized. This second step ensures consistent and accurate information, which leads to inventory optimization in the following ways:

- Possible duplicate parts can be identified. Redundant parts can be eliminated and inventories reduced
- Improved accuracy ensures the right part is selected every time
- Everyone has access to the same information
- Improved tracking ability means better forecasting
- Better planning reduces overstocking, false stock outs, and excessive shipping costs
- Procurement personnel can order MRO parts proactively, thus taking advantage of strategic pricing agreement

Integrated Maintenance and Procurement Planning

Once the required master data is ready, the organization can assess the current state of planning processes, implement a well-defined process for annual and periodic maintenance planning based on reliability-centered practices, and ensure that the processes are followed by planning teams. Annual and periodic maintenance planning will be one of the inputs for annual and periodic inventory category planning. Benefits delivered under this approach include:

- Improved demand visibility, enabling procurement to obtain the right part at the right time—at the best possible price and terms.

- Improved inventory planning, resulting in more appropriate total inventory investment.

- Improved service levels in areas such as parts availability at lower cost.

- Improved category planning and reduced cost of procurement.

Dispose of Unused and Obsolete Stock

An inventory planning team can identify obsolete items by coordinating with the asset management team and periodically tag the identified parts. Similarly, the inventory planning team can also identify and assess with end-users non-moving parts for future use to tag such parts in the system. Once the non-moving and obsolete parts are identified, the teams can analyze the physical condition of the parts, markets where these could be sold, and supplier buy-back options and accordingly inform the customer to initiate appropriate action.

Risk Management

Risk is broadly, a potential to loss. Loss can be due to contract risks or due to work execution at site. While it is important to minimize the potential risks of your contracts, it's also important that you don't miss great opportunities for the fear of risk. Like hockey legend Wayne Gretzky said, "You miss 100% of the shots you don't take."

Considering Risk as a product of severity and probability, it needs to be Identified evaluated & Mitigated to the possible extent.

Different Types of Risks

Major Risks	Risk Factors
External and site condition Risks	• Unforeseen site conditions. • Weather Condition • Difficult in obtaining permits and ordinances. • Changes in government actions
Economical & Financial Risks	• High Inflation/Increased Price • Delayed payments on contract • High Interest rate • Poor cost control
Technical and contractual Risks	• Defective Design • Design change by Owner • Inadequate compensation for activity • Delay in arranging documents or resources
Managerial Risks	• Improper maintenance work or monitoring • Low labour productivity • Problem with resource mobilization • Inadequate Spares & Shutdown

Risks, as in Site Operations

Maintenance risk may refer to the risk of improper maintenance resulting in a lack of performance, which is implicit and covered in availability and performance risk analysis.

But maintenance risk also refers to the risk of higher costs for maintenance operations and plans (including current maintenance and life-cycle costs). This is the focus of the risk in this section.

This is also a general and natural risk to be allocated to the service provider, as the maintenance obligation is a core element of contract scope.

The risk may correlate with the design risk, as improper design may lead to higher maintenance costs, especially major maintenance and renewals (life-cycle costs), which is a risk generally transferred by default to the private partner.

In this sense, not only can design influence the life cycle of the infrastructure, but also renewals and major maintenance carried out in past. These should be handled in advance through adequate planning (programming the cycle of renewals so as to avoid, as much as possible, interruption of the service or its availability), This is also a concern for the customer who will usually request a budget approval plan for maintenance works and the creation of contingency funds for unanticipated needs.

Lastly, the risk refers to ordinary maintenance costs (ad hoc small repairs, restoration of painting, recurrent cleaning, and so on). Some ordinary maintenance tasks are confused or overlap with certain services and other cost concepts that may not be considered as maintenance, but which may also be included in the maintenance concept.

"First and foremost, Site managers must prevent threats to human health and safety that can arise from poorly maintained life safety equipment, improper handling of hazardous materials and other workplace issues. "Beyond physical risks, however, companies must also heed new financial, reputational and contractual risks. The cost of non-compliance can be severe and even material."

As compliance issues continue to increase in priority for site managers, to monitor and keep tap on to avoid penalties that can negatively impact your organization.

Ethics. Aside from being potentially illegal, unethical behavior can have negative consequences for both a company's bottom line and reputation. For that reason, a facility management service provider should demonstrate a strong commitment to ethical behavior that includes, for instance, the obligation to refuse gifts from any kind for subcontractor.

Safety. From maintenance of fire extinguishers to safe handling of hazardous waste, physical security is not only a top priority, but also a highly visible area of compliance risk and legal liability. And, company environmental health and safety (EHS) policies and procedures can help reduce incident risk.

Vendor and financial management. For companies, particularly those that outsource facilities management, appropriate internal financial controls and management are essential for service providers and their subcontractors for ethics compliance. Strictly enforced procurement and vendor management policies and procedures can reduce the risk.

Labor management. Companies must ensure their Site managers, whether in-house or outsourced providers, comply with anti-discrimination laws, other human resource-related regulations and company policies not only in their own operations, but also with their subcontractors.

Information security. Many high-profile data breaches have occurred because of physical security weaknesses. The importance of these processes is elevated for companies using smart building management services or integrating corporate data into the provider's data and analytics platforms. Companies should confirm that their service providers are equipped to protect both physical and virtual corporate data assets with best practices and access control.

Data governance. When a company is fully compliant, its data should reflect it. Even the most robust investments in compliance will not pay off if regulatory agencies can't access the information they need, when they demand it. Site management teams must standardize the data related to compliance and ensure that it is accurate, consistent, timely, complete and secured.

Contractual risks: Breach of contract is a financial and legal risk where even a minor infraction can have serious repercussions. If an Service provider fails to maintain systems properly in accordance with its master service agreement, the resulting equipment breakdown could jeopardize operations.

VIEWPOINT

- Total service provider experience in discipline/industry is not the horizontal sum of different people in team but vertical depth of industrial knowhow. As battery in parallel add on the current, whereas in series adds on potential.

Chapter 10

Claims & Alignment

"There are only two things in a business that make
money—innovation and marketing, everything else is cost."

– Peter Drucker

As by now, we must accept the objective of outsourcing activity as slashing costs with improved productivity. Outsourcing has been now adopted by different industries for a wide range of functions from Human resources, Account function, IT services, Facility maintenance, etc. which may directly does not impact the product quality but Cost and productivity remain a major concern.

Although the idea of outsourcing the production equipment maintenance comes with a lot of concerns and a wide variety of myths. Myths – Not sound perfect as customer and Service provider both are well conversant of the subject, difference whatever exists is about their business model and priorities. The term "Claim and Alignment" in such a case sounds more appropriate. Claim here stands for mean position and Alignment is somewhat a deviation from the mean.

Normally outsourcing started from non-core activities and extended to the entire range of function with quality control and marketing being the only core activity. This is now very commonly adopted practice at different manufacturing facility used for manufacturing different brands of product and optimizing the cost most common in luminaries manufacturing, textile manufacturing, etc.

On the other hand, it is also very true every single activity toward backward integration gives better control over the cost and quality of the system. It is a balance between two that decide the ideal mix. Analysis and decision taking on the same have been already discussed in a separate chapter.

1. **Claim** – Service organization sometimes claims "Maintenance" as a profit center instead of a cost center.

   Alignment – Maintenance is profit centre for service agency only. It is always a cost centre for manufacturing unit and remains to be same, unless expenses reduced down beyond zero making it negative. To make it into profit center cost of maintenance should turn negative, where it starts generating revenues and can be categorized at a profit center in the true term.

   The maintenance can turn into a profit center when it's limit is extended beyond zero and is possible in some specific cases where the maintenance team develops competency and infrastructure to extent of supporting other industries in addition to fulfilling their own in-house requirement forming a source of revenues. i.e. motor workshop in any industry provides services to other nearby industries.

   Another example can be from any industry with captive power plant and maintenance team work out the energy-saving plans leading to substantial saving in energy without affecting productivity and that additional energy can be made available to grid adding up the revenues.

2. **Claim** – Salesperson does not need a product or system knowledge.

   Alignment – This can be limited to the extent of product sales, but in case of services and if it involves Equipment and engineering knowledge than salesperson needs to have a fair knowledge of plant equipment and process to understand the customer pain points and realistic way to optimize the same. It is also noticed, lack of subject understanding even at the back office makes them appear more like an additional customer demanding more explanation instead of supporting a site team.

3. **Claim** – OEM is always a better service provider for a maintenance contract.

   Alignment – OEM can be a better service provider if is an expert in specific industrial process engineering with specialization in a product line. Equipment OEM with limited system knowledge may not meet customer expectations, although charges premium for average services. The Customer should access the service provider capability and his requirement.

4. **Claim** – All contract under a single umbrella is effective and optimum.

   Alignment – Every added subcontract under the umbrella of the main contract weakens the governance and causes leakage of cost. These decisions are to be analyzed thoroughly.

5. **Claim** – Outsourcing maintenance would be an admission of internal failure.

   Alignment – This is not the case as owning a special tool and skill for some time in the future which may or may not be required continuously, can be a costly proposition with loss of effectiveness. While on the other side it would make business sense for a service provider based on the economy of scale and optimum utilization of resources with a continuous technology upgrade.

6. **Claim** – Control on maintenance activities are somewhat weakened.

   Alignment – This usually depends upon establishing the level of communication between customer and service provider. Actually, to extract maximum out of such contracts, both should act in synergy toward deriving the common objective. Lack of such association leads to a lot of disruption with conflicts and non-acceptability of each other.

In the case of maintenance outsourcing service providers should be very well conversant with the manufacturing process and different controls to ensure optimal productivity of the plant. Maintenance contractors cannot be mavericks doing their own things.

Maintenance contractors must be able to present performance matrices and maintenance data to justify the contract and to demonstrate the continuous improvement plan in place.

In case of deviations in achieved results, there should certainly be a time-bound action plan to improve the condition and needs to be properly documented.

7. **Claim**-Contractor is responsible and accountable to maintain the entire plant and should bear penalties on account of non-attainment of KPI equating to loss made in the manufacturing process.

   Alignment – This is moreover depending upon the customer requirement and signed contract between two parties. The contract should clearly define the responsibility with the extent of degrees to avoid such misunderstanding.

   On the customer side, it should be clear, unlimited liability is not even included in Insurance which is on high premium and is taken out without involving in any activities with assumptions of ideal practices in place.

8. **Claim** – In the case of outsourced maintenance, no internal expertise is built-in and experienced persons would feel of being underutilized.

   Alignment – Ideally internal specialization requirement is minimized with a reduction in associated cost, which anyway remains the objective of an organization. An experienced person can be utilized to guide and monitor the contractor with free himself for other necessary activities towards modification, energy-saving opportunity, and optimized utilization of resources.

Maintenance contractors due to their broad access to maintenance technologies and best practices will actually enhance the capabilities of current workers. Most contractors have necessary training programs for their employees that not only expand the technical capabilities of a team but also improve on other skills necessary for the successful execution of maintenance in the contractor environment.

9. **Claim** – Maintenance can be improved faster and better by using internal resources.

Alignment – This shall not be the case for activity not having any financial implication. In case of financial implication inertia of Service provider organization and hierarchy, structure will add up to customer internal processes.

As maintenance is an emergency requirement, a service provider with localized control at the site with limited hierarchy is always an advantage.

Organizational with analytics in decision making is a better choice instead of industries adopting old school practices, HIPPO (High paid person opinion).

In the normal course, making significant improvements in maintenance requires focusing on the entire process instead of individual activity. The maintenance process basically comprises of six elements as:

 a. People

 b. Leadership

 c. Spare parts

 d. Tools and technology

 e. Processes

 f. Costs

 g. Safety

As maintenance is not core activity in most of the manufacturing industry they are acquired with limited knowledge on the subject and internal resources. Maintenance being a core business of service provider is better placed in terms of knowledge and resources on account of the economy of scale. Flexibility is an additional advantage in the case of an outsourcing partner. As hiring different skills, replacing existing team members, arranging special tools when required is comparatively difficult with the internal process.

8. **Claim** – Outsourcing maintenance will significantly increase the maintenance cost

   Alignment – Outsourcing maintenance will somewhat increase the cost on account of logistics i.e. duplication of resources in terms of Safety, Security, conveyance, administration, etc. Need to keep a close tap on service provider back-office administration cost, project management cost, etc. which directly not impact maintenance effectiveness. On the other side outsource service providers can leverage the cost on account of the economy of scale due to multiple clientele base and cost reduction by improving process efficiency. Effective maintenance shall always:

   - Reduce breakdowns
   - Reduce the equipment lifecycle cost.
   - Cost reduction by optimizing the redundant equipment.
   - Improve employee customer and employee satisfaction.
   - Reduces scrap and waste.
   - Positively impacts the safety and lost time.

   The benefits of cost-saving on the above points along with value addition in different points can definitely surpass the slight increase in cost and further possibility of cost reduction by sharing resources i.e. Conveyance facility, Security, HR support in handling local issues can be effective.

There will be many claims with multiple justifications between customer and service provider. The key to success lies in understanding the requirement to the best possible extent framing into suitable contract accepting limitations and driving synergy towards raising the performance Benchmark.

The decision to outsource or not is a complex one and to be analyzed to all possible combinations with possibilities. Adding too much of unforeseen risks or stringent KPI shall add up the maintenance cost on one hand and non-attainment of the same will cause de-motivation in the team. Every case and customer is different and to be analyzed accordingly.

For Example, a small manufacturing unit with advanced level automation and lean manpower outsourcing to a few automation system experts is an ideal choice. In the case of the continuous process plant with more than 5 in nos. at a different location, it shall be an ideal choice for having their own centralized maintenance department with all competency within the team. Visit based service contracts can be fixed with experts for specialized services.